"A good conversation can shift
the direction of change forever"

—— **Would you leave it to chance?**

BIS Publishers
Borneostraat 80-A
1094 CP AMSTERDAM
The Netherlands
T +31(0)20 515 02 30
bis@bispublishers.com
www.bispublishers.com

Published by Event Design Collective GmbH
www.eventcanvas.org

Authors:
Roel Frissen, Ruud Janssen, Dennis Luijer

Visual Storyline Development:
Dennis Luijer

Co-contributor:
Paul Rulkens

Editor:
John Loughlin

Audio Book Narration:
Anthony Vade

Design & Layout:
Cristel Lit, Giovanni de Reus, Frank Bakker

ISBN 978 90 636 9680 1

DESIGN
to Change

Elevating your abilities
to look and act beyond the now

Roel Frissen | Ruud Janssen | Dennis Luijer

Co-contributor: Paul Rulkens

EVENT DESIGN *collective*

B/S

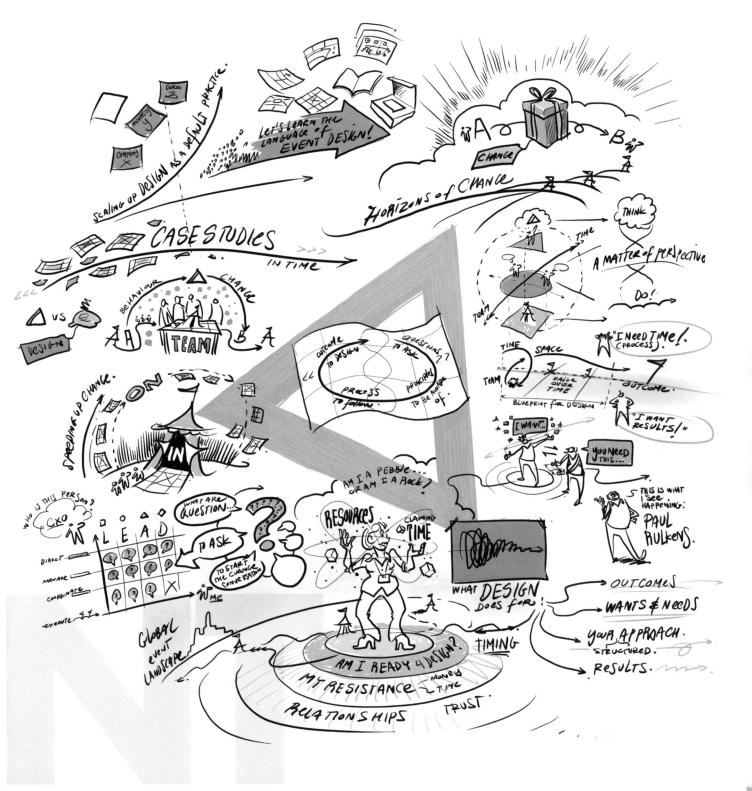

After Michelangelo finished the magnificent statue of David, people asked him how he had created such a masterpiece. Michelangelo answered that he envisioned the David hidden inside the raw block of marble, after which he simply took out everything which was not David.

Often the way to improve a product or a service is not to try to add things, but simply take out everything which masks its brilliance. Design to Change is therefore about how to focus on what matters in event design, while at the same time remove the irrelevant, distracting, and confusing.

The most impactful event I have attended in my life was in a repurposed exercise room in a center for the elderly. The most sophisticated tool in the room was a flip-chart. Home-made lemonade was served in cardboard cups. Yet, the entire afternoon was gripping and engaging, and many months afterwards, the impact of the event still reverberated in the company.

I believe that the best events are part of a process which facilitates long term improvement. If it doesn't, it's not an event, but entertainment.

I also believe there is a method to the madness in event design. Success is predictable and follows a pattern. If we understand this pattern, we can improve.

"There is a method to the madness"

There are two big mistakes that are often made in event design. The first mistake occurs when the purpose of the event is to impress others. As a result the event is focused on meticulous stage craft, overwhelming sensory stimulus, and a general feeling of massive wow. All of this is nice, but it could also be achieved by hiring a magician. Often with a much lower price tag as well.

The second mistake occurs when the sole purpose of the event is to entertain the audience. This creates a momentary rush of energy, happiness, and well being. It also fades away soon after the event.

What I have learned instead as a corporate executive, and later in my career as a professional speaker, is that any event should improve the condition of the person or entity which pays for the event. This could be a corporate event resulting in Behavioural change, or a client event resulting in additional sales.

After every chapter, Paul Rulkens will provide his Executive Perspective.

PAUL RULKENS
TRUSTED ADVISOR

An effective event designer has therefore one question on top of their mind: How will this event improve the condition of the client? Actual event benefits, such as higher revenue, more engagement, or a better place to work, transform any event from being a cost item to a critical investment.

This book provides the necessary perspectives, ideas, and tools to make this shift. It's written without adding unnecessary clutter, which would only water down its value.

If you want to improve, it's not so much about adding stuff. "It's about focusing on the few things which matter, and at the same time getting rid of everything which masks your strengths."

Are you ready to create a David masterpiece of your own?

ABOUT ME

Paul Rulkens is an expert in high performance: the art and science of achieving big goals with the least amount of effort. He is an award-winning professional speaker, author and a trusted boardroom advisor who has helped thousands of business owners, professionals and executives get everything they can out of everything they have.

Originally trained as a chemical engineer, Paul's work is based on deep knowledge and extensive experience in the practical business applications of Behavioural psychology, neuroscience and, especially, common sense.

As a corporate leader he has worked more than 20 years on the frontline of global business. This makes him both a scholar and a strategist and provides his clients with a unique mix of scientific insights and proven, pragmatic help.

His popular TEDtalks, which have been watched more than four million times on YouTube, are used frequently in professional training sessions all over the world.

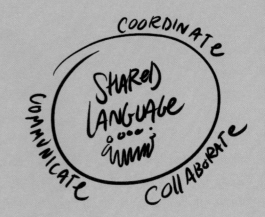

LOOK AND ACT BEYOND THE NOW

—————— INTRODUCTION

In 2016 we published our first book, Event Design Handbook, in which we explained in detail a powerful methodology to design events. The handbook describes a specific framework called the Event Canvas used to analyse the effect of past events and to design purposeful future events. The Event Canvas and its related tools proved to be well-received and well-implemented by event designers and we are encouraged by the success our users are having with the model and of the book. But we have discovered that as event designers have come to embrace the canvas for its analytical methodology and its strategy management, there is still more to master. Additionally, not every stakeholder understands the value of investing in event design in the first place. This book will detail that value.

11

Although it arrives more than four years later, this book is not a follow-up to the Event Design Handbook. And it is not a prequel. It comes not before or after the 2016 book in terms of its concepts. It is instead a companion piece. You do not need to have read either book first in order to understand the other.

The Event Design Handbook defines and describes the implementation of the Event Canvas in detail as the tool for event design. That same tool is embedded in this book. If you begin your journey into event design with that book, you can familiarize yourself with the Event Canvas first and then extend your reach for value, execution, and communication with this one. Alternately, you can read this book first to understand the value of design and the need to coordinate operations for that value; and then afterwards dig deeper into the specific utilization of the Event Canvas tool with the Event Design Handbook. Reading either book, or both in either order, the reader will better understand how events can be integral to and planned into any organization's short-term and long-term goals.

The primary tools for the process of Event Design are explained in detail in Event Design Handbook—like the central tool of the Event Canvas itself, Stakeholder Alignment, the Empathy Map, the LEAD model, and looking back-looking forward, among others. In this book you will find additional tools that both build on and support those in Event Design Handbook. One purpose for introducing companion tools here is to advance the practice of Event Design for those who already employ the Event Canvas. Another purpose is to elevate the practice of Event Design by examining why the methodology is so essential. The main purpose of this book is to empower anyone to invite others, in conversations, to coordinate, collaborate, and communicate with a common, deliberate methodology, a unified understanding, and a shared language.

This book is for anyone interested in how events can create value for an organization. This includes people in any way connected to a designed event: designers, owners, managers, gatekeepers, in the conversations they are having.

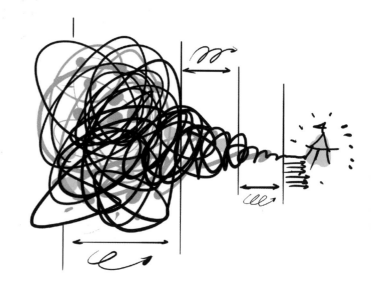

EVENT

Any gathering of two or more people or groups of people that changes behaviour.

EVENT DESIGN

The process of articulating change, setting boundaries, and prototyping your events using design thinking and doing.

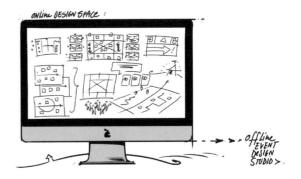

EVENT CANVAS ™

A visual-thinking tool on a single piece of paper that allows people to articulate how an event creates value. The Event Canvas ™ was developed by Roel Frissen and Ruud Janssen and can be studied further at eventcanvas.org

EVENT DESIGN STUDIO

Event Design Studio: A online or offline space in which the Event Design Team applies the Event Design using the Event Canvas™ methodology.

MAPPING THE STAKES.

PARK ALL IDEAS HERE UNTIL PHASE II (PROCESS FIRST!)

CHOOSING WHOM TO DELIGHT

EMPATHISE + IN-OUT + FRAME (CHANGE)

EVENT DELTA [ARTICULATING THE DESIGN GOAL].

IDEA QUARANTINE

▷ STAKES

LONGLIST

▷ STAKEHOLDER ALIGNMENT

▷ CHOICE

EMPATHY   EVENTCANVAS™

PHASE I

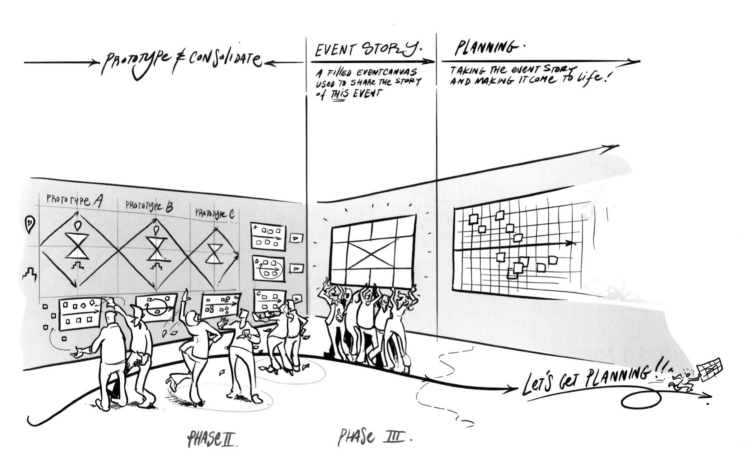

PROTOTYPE & CONSOLIDATE

EVENT STORY.
A FILLED EVENTCANVAS USED TO SHARE THE STORY OF THIS EVENT

PLANNING.
TAKING THE EVENT STORY AND MAKING IT COME TO LIFE!

PROTOTYPE A   PROTOTYPE B   PROTOTYPE C

LET'S GET PLANNING!!

PHASE II.   PHASE III.

WHO IS IT FOR?

1) Event Owners:

When you lead an organisations' change, you realize that events can be a strong agent of change. The financial, organisational and risk implication for the organization means that owning the event can be a daunting prospect. Being the Event Owner puts you at the core of these decisions. Their success can make or break your reputation and that or your organization and brand.

This book is equally for those who are not directly responsible for design, but are stakeholders in an event or series of events. It will first introduce the extraordinary value of design and help you understand what all designers are so obsessed about when suggesting event design.

TOMORROW

2) Event Designers not familiar with the Event Canvas:
This book is also intended for people who work in event design but who are not themselves well-versed in the process of designing for behaviour change through events, and for people who have never considered how and why a designed event can achieve a single, specified goal, or multiple, intended organizational goals. For event designers not yet familiar with the Event Canvas, this book will open the world of possibility to structured and strategic event design and by doing so serve as a primer for learning how to use the Canvas.

3) Event Designers familiar with the Event Canvas:
People who are already familiar with and dedicated to using the Event Canvas and other related tools will find new layers of insight here. For the event designer already familiar with the Event Canvas, this book will provide concepts to take your use of this tool even farther, and it will also provide you with communication strategies to attract others to the usefulness of claiming time, team tand space to design for more valuable outcomes.

This book will be redundant for you if:

☐ **YOU CAN ARTICULATE CLEARLY YOUR LONG- AND SHORT-TERM GOALS AND KNOW HOW EVENTS CAN SUCCESSFULLY ACHIEVE THEM**

☐ YOU HAVE DETERMINED THE BEHAVIOUR CHANGES THAT WILL RESULT IN ACHIEVING YOUR GOALS

☐ you validated exactly how your events are perceived by your stakeholders

☐ **YOU LIKE DESIGN BUT NOT FOR YOUR EVENT**

☐ You have clearly defined jobs to be done and know how to get them done

☐ **YOU DON'T LIKE TO CHALLENGE THE STATUS QUO**

☐ YOU HAVE A COMMON LANGUAGE TO ADDRESS BEHAVIOUR CHANGE THROUGH EVENTS

☐ you are confident of handling any conversation around the above mentioned items at any time

Or are you ready to challenge your thinking?

SHARE

Share your questions, pictures and user generated content by using the hashtag #EventCanvas, which is used by your fellow event owners and event design practitioners across the globe.

Bring the visuals in this book to life by checking out **www.designtochange.online** and discover the conversations and animations online and in Augmented Reality.

WHAT'S TO COME

There are a handful of practical tools and concepts that we will go into in detail individually in later chapters. You might be listening to the audio book, swiping through a digital book or you have the analog book in your hands. Whichever the format, this content is complemented by a powerful digital twin. There you will find real life examples of conversations, collaborative tools and templates.

Concepts that will be explored in this book and online include:
- Stakeholder Alignment
- Perspective Analysis
- Past-Present-Future Evaluation
- Back-casting
- Claiming Time
- Claiming Space
- Presenting Prototypes instead of ideas
- Timing Conversations
- Becoming a Trusted Advisor

These tools, and others, will improve your interactions and output when you discover them in the first place, and then learn how they are honed and deliberate so that you can be, too.

Some tools constitute an entire chapter for itself, while other tools are defined and described within a chapter concept.

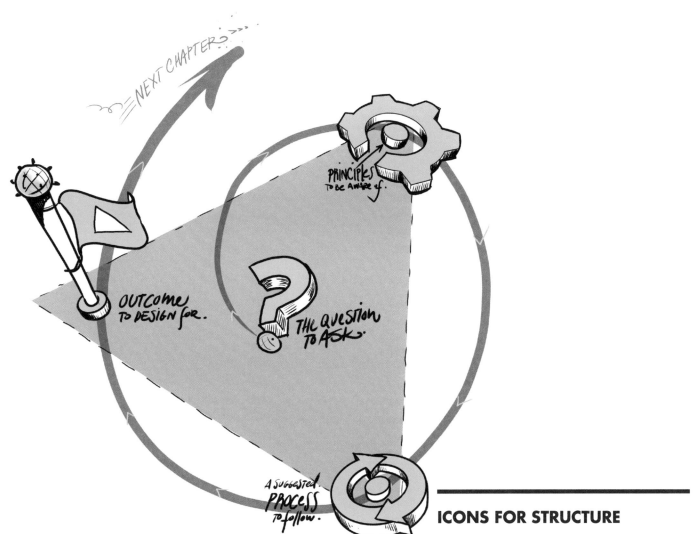

NEXT CHAPTER

PRINCIPLES
TO BE AWARE of.

OUTCOME
TO DESIGN for.

THE QUESTION
TO ASK.

A SUGGESTED
PROCESS
TO follow.

ICONS FOR STRUCTURE

Each chapter will introduce a basic four-part
structure. The icons will guide you along the way:

(?) Question to ask

(⚙) Principles

(◎) Process

(🏳) Outcome

23

Take a moment to reflect. Grab a pen.
Jot down the answers to the following questions:

What recent conversation did you have (that you left to chance) that you wish you could redo?

What would you do differently next time?

Take a Moment ... REFLECT.

How did it make you feel at the time?

01. HOR

HORIZONS OF CHANGE

QUESTION TO ASK

In this chapter, we will examine change, its potential for value, and its availability to be designed.

So, the pain question to ask: **Why is everyone (else) so reluctant to change?**
The gain question: **How do you understand change to create value?**

This is the most concise question to begin the conversation, but it leads to a cascade of follow-up questions:

- What is change?
- How does change become value?
- Can it really be designed?
- How is it designed?
- What are the tools?
- What are the obstacles in designing for change?
- Who wants it?
- Who does it target?
- Who designs it?
- Who should change?

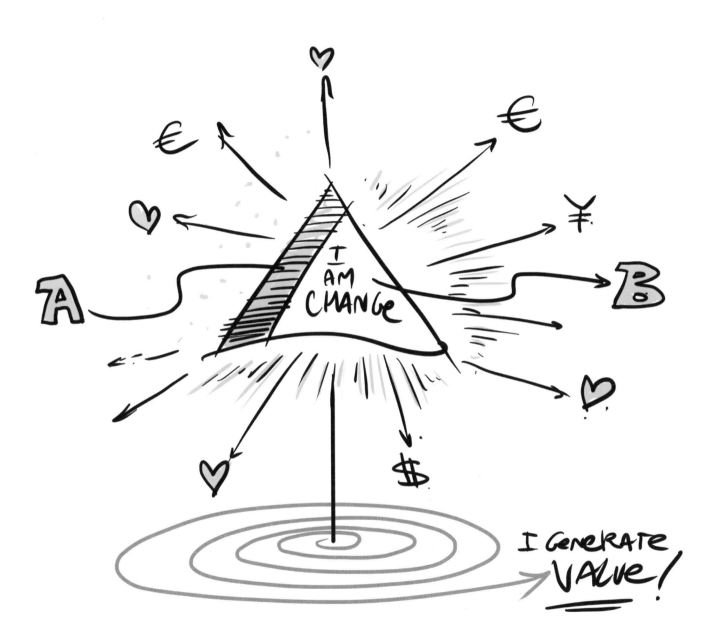

I AM CHANGE

A

B

I GENERATE VALUE!

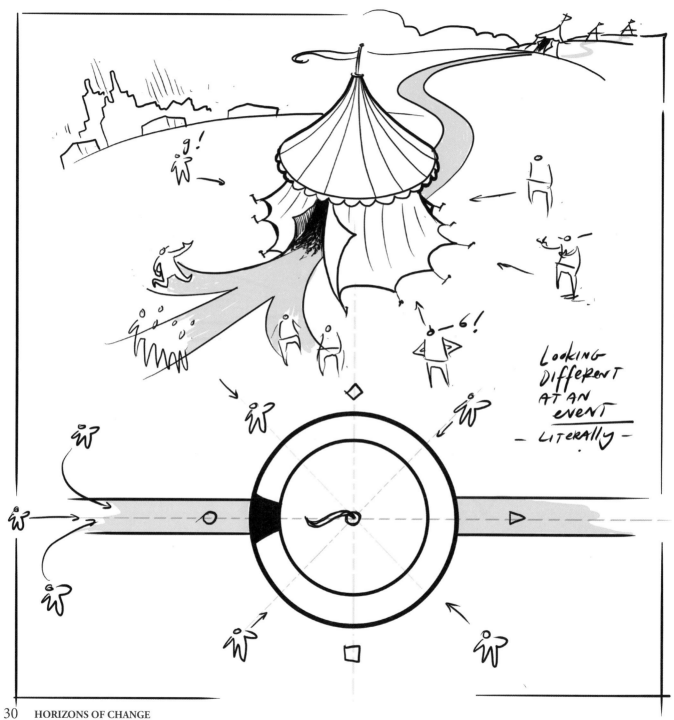

Looking
Different
At an
event
— Literally —

EVENT DELTA:

The intended change in behaviour of the key stakeholders as a result of attending an event.

PRINCIPLES

What is change, anyway? Change, on one hand, may seem obvious: a known thing transforms into something else. Change is perhaps the only constant in life, it is the experience of change that defines anything that happens to us. It is inevitable. And we're used to that.

But, on the other hand, change is difficult to define explicitly to ourselves and to others. It happens with or without our influence, with or without our attention, which means it is usually random.

However, we can we specify its meaning, usefulness, and properties. We use it as both a noun and a verb: We can change this; and Here is the change. It is used to describe something both internal and expressed externally as behaviour.

One way to understand what change means, it turns out, is implied in the final question in the list above: Why is everyone (else) so reluctant to change? This question reveals much about the nature of change because of what it means to people. The question acknowledges that change is internalized, an individual experience. It acknowledges that the experience of change is subject to perspective (I accept change, why won't they? They should change, why should I?). And it acknowledges that that individual experience of changing can be uncomfortable, especially if it is imposed. Understanding this discomfort and reluctance is integral to knowing how to design for it.

This dissonance between appreciating change (in the world and in others) and resisting change (in oneself) shows us what change is, by showing us what it means to the individual. The multiple perspectives to change turns out to be the key to examining something so hard to define otherwise.

Change means different things to different people at different times. By paying attention to this multitude of experiences we can begin to identify recurring aspects of the phenomenon of change. By identifying its commonalities across perspectives, we can define something so nebulous.

So, to further the Principles of this chapter about change, let's take a look at some singular aspects of change itself:
- Change happens over time: There is a before condition, and an after condition.
- Change is trackable: We can identify the before condition and the after condition; the difference between them is called the Delta.
- Change happens in increments: Often the visible change or desired change is the result of many smaller changes. This is when identifying Deltas becomes useful. You may be interested in one ultimate change to create value, but what incremental Deltas will it take for people to reach that end result? Planning for the ultimate value requires planning for Deltas along the way.
- Change only happens in the now: It is an action that can only happen in the present.
- Value comes from behaviour change: Internal change (new knowledge) is only valuable when it leads to external actions—behaviour change.
- Change from one event will be different for different people: Different stakeholders have different perspectives and so what they experience will also be different.
- The status quo is more comfortable than change: Perpetuating in the present what is familiar from the past is easier and safer than grappling with the unproven and the unknown future, whether it be planning for change in others or enacting change in oneself.
- But change happens, anyway.
- Being urged to change behaviour or deciding to make a change in one's own behaviour requires effort, dedication, and focus. But if someone's perspective changes first, then their behaviour change can follow more easily.
- Change together is more comfortable than change alone: People evaluate cues from others in their purview and seek alignment. Countless studies show that individuals will work against their own interest and even safety if they feel like an outlier.
- Behaviour change can be planned for: If you can analyse it, you can work with it.

So, now, if change can be identified, then it is also possible to craft change. Even though change is going to happen anyway, it can be guided. Can desired outcomes in behaviour change be planned for by designing an event? The simple answer is a resounding and exciting, Yes. Change can be bad, neutral, or good; it can be made good; and good change can be designed for with understanding and intention, coordination and communication.

So, what can be done to affect change? Events, for one. When we talk about events, we mean something both broad and specific. As we are social beings, interactions are inevitable and frequent, and they have consequences.

We define events as having two clear attributes. First, an event is a gathering of two or more people, or groups of people. Reading a book alone does not qualify as an event, but when you have a meeting with others to discuss ideas from this book, you may now have an event. That is, if the second criterion is met, which is that the two

or more people have something at stake. They choose to create, contribute to, or participate in a gathering because it is more important to them, for reasons of their own, to be involved than it is to not. As such, an event can be considered to be any gathering that is important enough to add to your schedule. That is to say, when a gathering affects the concerns of the participants, that is an event.

The really interesting aspect is that events elicit change. They affect people. Something changes in them. Maybe it's internal: their outlook, their understanding, their creativity, their intentions. But the ultimate significance of an event's effect is in the behaviour change of the participants—how behaviour changes from before the event, to after the event. And this change can be designed for.

This change in behaviour is trackable (and called the Delta). It's worth taking a hard look at how it can be measured and designed to change behaviour because change in behaviour is where value is created.

You may successfully seek the right audience and communicate your message to them. The information about your brand, or your cause, or a potential collaboration may reach them. They may receive and process it, but if they don't buy differently, participate differently, volunteer differently, donate differently, etc. then no value has been created. Well, at least no intended value has been created. Merely the status quo has been maintained and the only value is that negative change has been avoided. At least they've been reminded that your organization and its mission still exist. Or perhaps you can only hope to be lucky and have an event of random change that turns out to be beneficial. Happy accidents do occur every once in a while. But plannable value worth investing in, results only when change is designed to produce intended new actions.

These principles, and the tools in this book and in the Event Design Handbook, shape a methodology of understanding and action. By identifying and understanding discrete aspects of change, like the ones listed above, behaviour change can be planned for. By understanding change in such specific ways, the process of designing for change through events can be discussed with a common language, a common goal, and within a structured methodology. Furthermore, once that commonality is reached, the outcome can be divided into clear tasks which are delegated and sequenced over time.

Now that we have pinned down some aspects of change and the value of behaviour change, and proposed that events can achieve such valuable results, how does Event Design deliver them? We'll offer many tools throughout the chapters to come starting with Horizons of Change.

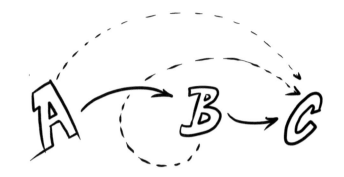

STANFORD ENCYCLOPEDIA OF PHILOSOPHY

Indicative Conditionals

A - Antecedent
B - Behaviour
C - Consequence

ABC MODEL

The Antecedent-Behaviour-Consequence (ABC) Model is a tool that can help people examine Behaviours they want to change, the triggers behind those Behaviours, and the impact of those Behaviours patterns. Rather than occurring in isolation, Behaviour is preceded by an antecedent (trigger) that sets off the Behaviour and is followed by a consequence, or a reaction to the Behaviour. This process is easily remembered by the acronym ABC.

EVENT DESIGN
MASTERMIND

INGRID RIP, CED+

DIRECTOR
EVENT DESIGN COLLECTIVE NETHERLANDS

It can be tempting to only think of the next most immediate event, but that can be short sighted. To truly have impact, stakeholders often need to achieve their (strategic) goals over a longer time span. Why is it hard to get this message across? After reading Design to Change, I realized that we often look at events from different perspectives and timelines. A valuable conversation requires you to be agile, able to switch perspectives. To really understand, so you can get conscious event design on the agenda.

———

NAOMI LOVE, CED, CMM

PROGRAM & EVENTS MANAGER

STANFORD UNIVERSITY | BECKMAN CENTER FOR MOLECULAR & GENETIC MEDICINE

Every waking moment is driven by human Behaviourism and changing Behaviour can be as simple as ABC (Antecedent/Behaviour/Consequence). The #EventCanvas is the tool that helps drive organizational change through the power of events. Once the language of Event Design is adopted, it quickly becomes a way of life. That language has positively impacted my day-to-day conversations. Conversations have been elevated and are more meaningful with my executive stakeholders, co-workers, suppliers, etc., pretty much EVERYONE! I am becoming a trusted advisor. I am forever changed & there is no turning back.

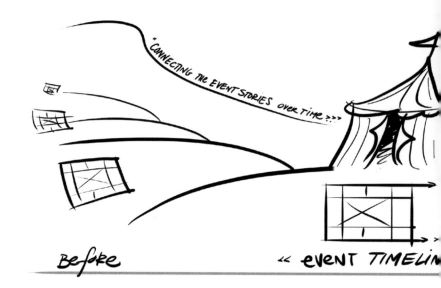

"CONNECTING THE EVENT STORIES OVER TIME >>>

Before   << event TIMELIN

PROCESS

The main tool with which to familiarize yourself to begin planning for change, or to communicate with others your designed event, is the concept of Horizons. Horizons of Change, the name of this chapter, refers to a way to think about the scale of change. A Horizon is the limit to how far you can see into the future and plan for change. Over the Horizon is the unknown; it lies beyond predictability and cannot be planned for. Most importantly, the Horizon defines a goal, and in so doing, aligns the collaborators. It needs to be determined in advance, communicated, and agreed to by all who strive for shared goals.

Of course, no one can see into the future, but it is possible to assess the effects of past events, identify trends, assess multiple aspects of the present, and anticipate how they will either continue or change. We have the great capacity to anticipate because we recognize patterns. Certainly, the future is full of surprises. Industrial giants

file for bankruptcy. A talented employee from a rival joins your team. A supply chain from abroad is disrupted. But to ameliorate the complete uncertainty of future events, we can apply what we have learned from past events and the patterns they draw.

We can analyse the past. We can organize the present. Therefore, we can design for the future. How far we are able to extend and guide identified patterns into the future is what sets the boundary of the Horizon. Designing for the future and using the concept of Horizons to do so is useful in many ways.

Discussing and defining the Horizon as a team creates better ideas because it channels multiple perspectives into a singular agreement about common goals. It creates team unity because the act of participating alongside peers generates enthusiasm and commitment. Moreover, setting out to define Horizons aligns people. It makes clear that

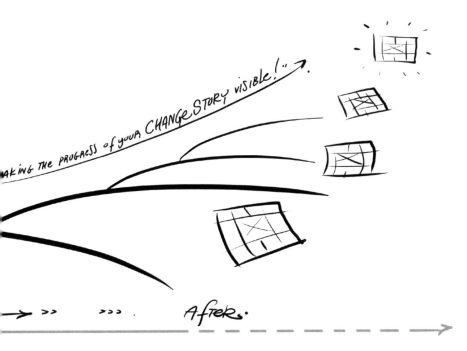

...AKING THE PROGRESS of your CHANGE STORY VISIBLE!...

After.

the group effort will be focussed as opposed to uniformed and with scattered efforts. Once a Horizon has been agreed to, different people can perform their varied tasks whilst still keeping to their common goal. Such alignment also produces more intelligent understanding of what is at stake according to the perspectives of stakeholders beyond the Horizon meeting.

Also critical to defining Horizons is that scale is necessarily flexible. One Horizon might be a five-year plan for growth. Yet within that plan is another Horizon: designing for the Delta of change along the way that is a specific Product Launch Event. And within that Horizon is another: aligning further colleagues, delivering design options, or winning approval.

Another Horizon within a five-year plan may extend only a single day, if that is how far you can see for the goal at hand: say, preparing results from Empathy Maps for a meeting tomorrow about the Framing step of the Event Canvas. There are different Horizons for different participants with different perspectives at different moments in their processes. But each defined Horizon is an essential tool to continually refer to because it aligns colleagues immersed in their different tasks, and acts as a reminder for any individual where they are in respect to the ultimate goal.

This takes us to a subsequent tool of the Horizons concept: Zoom In/Zoom Out. This refers to being adept at switching among different horizons throughout the design process, being clear about where you are, and making sure everyone else is shifting scope together. Communicating with the terms Zoom In and Zoom Out acknowledges several things: that there are different scales of focus; that there are identifiable increments of change along the path to more distant goals of behaviour changes; and that the concept of horizons provides the language to

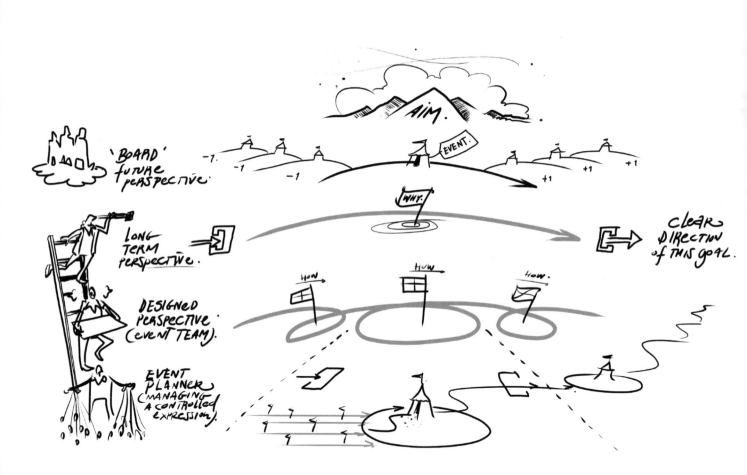

AIM.

EVENT

'BOARD' future perspective.

-1.   -1   -1   +1   +1   +1

WHY.

LONG TERM perspective.

CLEAR DIRECTION of this goal.

HOW   HOW   HOW.

DESIGNED perspective (event TEAM).

EVENT PLANNER (MANAGING A controlled expression).

communicate with colleagues about how the scope of the current horizon fits into other horizons.

By identifying Horizons and their scale in the first place, your teams can quickly align themselves with Zoom In/Zoom Out: Now we are zooming out to see how this summer's event fits into the five-year Horizon. Now we are zooming in to today's planning of next week's meeting, because of how it fits into the fundraiser (zooming out again).

It is like an online map application. You can see an image of the entire surface of the Earth and immediately know what you are looking at. But you also have the power to set your scale to study finer details. You can zoom in to a two-block sector of a neighbourhood in Buenos Aires and find street names, addresses, nearby businesses. Yet at the same time the edges of the map (the Horizon) become much closer: you can't see the big picture from here. But, you can zoom out again to see the land mass of South America. The edges of the map have expanded. You see the whole of a continent. But the refinement of fine details has become reduced. From this view, you can now only see general shapes: the land against the sea, broad political boundaries, basic geological features.

Each view is useful, and each is incomplete. You need them all. It's so essential to shift closer and further away from details within information that even paper maps have insets of different scale. Wonderfully, with digitized maps, you can immediately toggle through different scales of detail according to what it is you need to examine. The same is true within the flexibility of the human imagination in the form of Zoom In/Zoom Out when discussing Horizons of Change.

Being fluid with Zoom in/Zoom out is a relatively advanced skill that is more easily exercised after having already employed a methodological event design process a few times. It is best when it is second-nature, the way an experienced driver can shift a car's gears in the fraction of a second. When accelerating from a stop, when decelerating a little for a curve, or when decelerating completely for a red light, the operator has to know which way he's shifting, why, and how much, in anticipation of what he sees coming up ahead. And he has to know how to direct that shift without jamming the clutch. The same is true for steering your team through different Horizons. Zoom In/Zoom Out means shifting fluidly, with others, between different Horizons of Change.

Also, Zooming In and Zooming Out admits an additional concept, something from the principles section above: that change is incremental, that there are multiple Deltas. On the big roadmap, there are some select stops to chart along the way to your destination. Those individual Deltas must be quantified. That can be achieved by considering two variables: Amplitude and Frequency. Amplitude of Change is how much change is anticipated or achieved in a single event. Frequency of Change is when and how often the stepping stones of Deltas are planned. These two variables offer a way to simplify the conversation about the incremental Deltas within Horizons of Change. If you are having difficulty defining an ultimate Horizon and horizons within that, it will be useful to realign the team with Amplitude and Frequency. More on this in upcoming chapters with a pebble in a pond.

But for now: Change, Events, Horizons, Zooming In and Zooming Out. What do they deliver?

OUTCOME

First, by initiating conversation that specifically empha-sizes change, groups can identify goals and value, and can align themselves in their understanding and efforts to design for that value.

Second, know that you can design for change. The concept of Horizons highlights the grand principle that this is possible at all. The focus on a Horizon is one basic example that even something as nebulous as change can be delineated. If something can be quantified, it can be managed. Identifying commonalities among different ex-periences of change allows us to discuss it in detail, create a methodology about it, and scale it so that inter

mediate goals can be designed and tasks can be defined and delegated along the way.

Third, events are markers of change. A sequence of events planned to unfold over time toward an ultimate goal several Deltas, and therefore several Horizons. Event Design offers the tools to understand and process what has happened in the past, where the organization is in the present, and what will happen in the near future and distant future.

Finally, the twist. Change is required of you, too. It's something that will be a consistent theme of this book:

"Events are markers of change"

the value of behaviour change applies not just to target participants of a designed event, but to the diverse group of people themselves working to create that event. You're reading this book to improve what you do. And that is Change.

Change is the mother of value. Improvement requires change. But, as we've discussed, change can be uncomfortable. What are you trying to improve by adopting Event Design? Change in everyone else? Everyone (else) is reluctant to change. How about you? Are you resistant to change, yourself? Finding that will be an essential aspect in the next chapter about perspective and empathy.

Horizons, and its support tools of Zoom In/Zoom Out, and Amplitude/Frequency, constitute one part of the larger concept of Perspectives, which we will examine in whole in the next chapter. You may be in possession of a lens that can zoom in and zoom out, and you may even have mastered adjusting that scope. But there are others holding a different lens, in a different place, angled from a different altitude and distance. Who holds these different perspectives?

Why does the same thing look different to different people?

PAUL RULKENS

HORIZONS OF CHANGE

CHAPTER 01

If I organize an event, there are two things which are important to me.

First of all, I need to be able to express a vision.

The second thing , I need to be able to connect the vision to all participants and I need both. Because if I do not have a connection and I do not have a vision, I'm stuck.

If I do have a vision, but I don't make a connection, I'm operating in the ivory tower.

If I don't have a vision, but I have a great connection. This is typically what we call a kumbaya organization.

And finally, when I got a vision and I got a connection, this is how magic is being made.

So here's my question. If we talk about events and if we talk about horizons of change, what is it that we can do to ensure that people adopt the vision and don't simply see things?

At the same time, they connect to the vision in their own way, because this is the only way I will be able to drive change using the Horizon of Change.

Take a moment to reflect. Grab a pen.
Jot down the answers to the following questions:

How do you involve others in the change you design for?

How do you have that conversation with your event owner?

How do the events you design become markers of change in your organisation?

How do you enable them to express their vision?

How do you articulate the value it creates ?

How do you enable them to connect the vision to the event story?

02.

A MATTER OF PERSPECTIVE, A WAY OF LOOKING

PER

SPECTIVE

49

QUESTION TO ASK

A common frustration for collaborators is that others do not see what you have carefully considered. Others re-introduce ideas that you have analysed and wisely dismissed. They question basic principles that you have tested and identified as fundamental. They are disinterested in or do not follow your explanations. They insist on ideas that fail to meet what you understand to be the goal.

The pain question in this chapter is: **Why don't others see it like I do?**

The gain question is: **How can we as a group harness multiple perspectives?**

Be watchful when you think about the terms other and they. To everyone else, you are also they. Your insight may be researched and trail-blazing, but you are not the only thinker in the room. There is no alignment of one. You cannot lead alone and without input. Successful leaders know this. Reciprocal empathy is the answer, and it is practiced in the analysis of Perspective.

51

Perspective

| pə'spɛktɪv | noun

1a. A view or vista.
1b. A mental view or outlook.
2. The appearance of objects in depth as observed by normal binocular vision.
3a. The relationship of aspects of a subject to each other and to a whole.
3b. Subjective evaluation of relative significance; a point of view.
3c. The ability to perceive things in their actual inter-relations or comparative importance.
4. The technique of representing three-dimensional objects and depth relationships on a two-dimensional surface.

PRINCIPLES

Other stakeholders, by definition, have a different way of seeing and evaluating, and their perspectives are equally valid. So, it is in your best interest to acquire the skills to anticipate, understand, honour, and integrate the perspectives of others.

In this chapter we will examine how being aware of and understanding others' perspectives empowers you to create events that are meaningful to others, but also gives you the skills to present ideas in such a way that your innovations can reach others. So, first, let's define perspective.

To begin a dissection of the definition above, let's focus on the ones relating to the image of a physical object, definition parts 2 and 4. Although our point is not about being able to draw with skill, but rather mastering in-person communication, there are some applicable details within the pictorial definitions, and they give us a good place to start.

There is something called canonical perspective. If you were asked to draw a cube you would probably draw something like this:

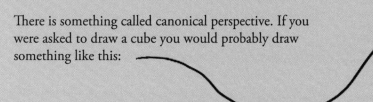

Almost everyone produces such a depiction. This is the canonical perspective: to the side, and slightly from above. When people are asked to draw a coffee cup or a chair, they draw as if standing from remarkably similar points of view: to the side, and slightly from above. The canonical perspective is common because it depicts our shared idea of an object, even though it is being translated from the real-world three-dimensionality of bulky planks of wood in space into an artifice of pencil strokes in two dimensions. Somehow, we all see the flattening of a cube in this particular way.

Even though the drawing is flat, its perspective implies that there is an object of depth and volume. There are multiple unseen sides. The canonical perspective satisfies definition 3a, that 'The relationship of aspects of a subject to each other and to a whole'.

It is still a legitimate angle of view of a cube, but the drawing from this perspective does not include the object's many aspects, their relation to each other, or to the whole. Its 'cubeness' is absent. All there is to see is a square. Two people can look at the same Rubik's cube from different perspectives and draw the single side of the square that they see—one person draws the green side, the other the white side. Within these two separate drawings of squares there is no indication that they relate to each other, or that there is a cube at all. The canonical perspective exists because it is more successful at depicting an object's essence.

In canonical perspective, such alignment just seems to be either hard-wired into our visual cortex or is the product of a cultural literacy we have acquired collectively. It represents the ideal: alignment in point of view. The viewer immediately comprehends the meaning of the drawing, and it is what was intended by the illustrator. But it is important to remember that it is incomplete, and not the only one. This is how it becomes relevant to our interests in innovation design.

Because, unfortunately, when it comes to abstractions, like ideas, purposes, meetings, events, etc., alignment is not so automatic. There is no canonical perspective on deltas of behaviour change. It takes intention and time, wisdom and practice, to align multiple perspectives. It takes understanding. It takes conversation. It takes empathy.

A perspective on something abstract is difficult to make concrete. Why did you like, or not, the last movie you saw? If you are concise, you disregard complexity. Or you are not concise, hunting for words because you are hunting for clarity. Yet even if you find the words to explain exactly why this was the best movie in the history of cinema, there is someone else in the room who feels the opposite.

Perspective is individual and internal. When shared, it flows from the inside out. Because perspectives come from an internal source, people push and defend them. Passion is the same thing, just with rocket fuel propelling it. People adhere to what they've processed to be true as 'The Truth' and can have negative reactions to the differing truth of another: feeling confused, insulted, misunderstood, pushed aside, frustrated, alone. People become entrenched. Opinions become even more set, perhaps now more loud, or now more silent, private, internal. This is misalignment and it is corrosive.

There is a way out of the destructive cycle, and it is to recognize: because abstract concepts are complex, varying perspectives are both valid and to be expected. While any one perspective of a concept may be true, it is likely not the complete truth. Your drawing does not show the other side of the cube. Someone else sees the far side, though. Multiple perspectives are in fact a resource. The fact that we look at the same thing creates value. Multiple brains considering the same concern from different perspectives produce better and more creative ideas. Perspectives

should be understood, embraced, celebrated, integrated. Everybody has a piece of the puzzle. This is a lesson in how to see that multiple squares make the cube.

In Event Design, perspective is the short-hand term that describes the fact that a single event can be looked at in different ways. Managing perspective is the ability to shift point of view to better understand what is different and valuable in other stakeholders, whether they be clients or colleagues, and conversely encourage them to better understand you.

Take a look at the sketch of the two people examining an object on the ground between them. One thinks it's a 6 and one thinks it's a 9. They are looking at the same thing from different perspectives. They see different things, and yet neither is wrong. Furthermore, there is still room for agreement. They can describe the shape and size, that it stands a certain height above the ground. It is a cipher of sorts, similar to but definitely not the letter g. The cipher represents something. Six means something, and nine means something too. Different, but equally meaningful.

One of the people might even happen to be adept at shifting perspective. Mr. 6 can walk around to the other side and see the object from Ms. 9's perspective, discover new meaning, and engage himself with the other. And in doing so, he can communicate with Ms. 9 in ways that invite him, in turn, to engage with the perspective of 6. "Ah, yes. I see your 9. Can you see my 6? It's right over here."

Please take a look at the drawing of an organization collaborating to deliver a series of events. It depicts four variables (in perspective, both pictorially and narratively). Different figures occupy different roles. The timeline of events at ground level extends into the distance. There are different scales of detail along that timeline. And there is a hierarchy: there are tiers of perspective at different altitudes from ground level and distances from events, depicted as tents as in the Event Design Handbook. Despite all the different perspectives, there are two critical connecting details depicted in the drawing: different heights run parallel to each other along the timeline into the Horizon, and the tiers are linked to each other by ladders. Everyone is looking at the same thing, seeing something different, but having good conversations with respect for each other's point of view.

THE VARIABLES OF PERSPECTIVE

As shown in the drawing, there are a few variables to a stakeholder's angle of view that determine role-specific perspective: Stake, Altitude, Scope (Zoom In/Zoom Out), and When. There is some overlap between them, but they are still able to be discerned.

1. Stake

As mentioned above, different stakeholders in an event will inherently see an event in different ways. These differences shape the way each stakeholder evaluates and communicates about results. But the overarching goal can be made common with Horizons of Change. The empathy to embrace and integrate multiple stakes is found in Event Design Handbook tools, like the Stakeholder Alignment exercise and making a shortlist of stakeholders to delight.

Furthermore, the stake someone has in an event is usually presented as a want. Most stakeholders are able to verbalise to some degree what it is they want as a result of an event. This is an expression of their perspective and should be welcomed as such. However, wants are incomplete. What it is that stakeholders truly need must be discovered. Needs are more elusive, harder to identify and verbalise. Yet needs are the outcomes more pertinent to individual stakeholders and are the more accurate and actionable specification of their perspective. Chapter four covers Wants versus Needs in greater detail.

2. Altitude

Altitude describes how close a person is to an event, but also includes their perspective within a hierarchy. Event owners, change owners, executives, and designers will see the same event, or series of events, from different altitudes. Some will see events from above, as only a discreet part of the organization's mission. While others, designers perhaps, will see events from ground level, as the defining objects and measures of the mission.

Designers, for example, exercise their jobs on tiers closer to the ground and concentrate their efforts on the narrative of an event. They become intimately informed of and invested in, the factors that make up the event and the process of its design.

On the other hand, executives use events as one tool among many to progress the interests of the organization. They are distanced from the design process and examine the event from a distance during its preparation, until they decide to focus on it, which is often the case when the event is about to happen.

And the participants of an event will see it differently still. Though it is their Behaviour change that is the intent of the event, they are not part of the design team.

We will focus our attention on interactions with the people who collaborate successfully, or not, during the planning and analysis of a future event's success. Design teams attend to the narrative of the event, while executives will consider events in the broad picture of intended change. This difference in altitude can lead to collaborative conflicts.

The conflicts pertain mostly to the level detail, available time, and desired results. Designers will spend the majority of their time addressing behaviour change using the Event Canvas. They will hold regular design sprints to analyse, design, and prototype. This is Process thinking and occurs at the ground-level altitude perspective.

On the other hand, at higher altitudes, executives will limit their involvement in the process of designing events. Perhaps they can only schedule time for occasional short briefings to check in on the design team's progress.

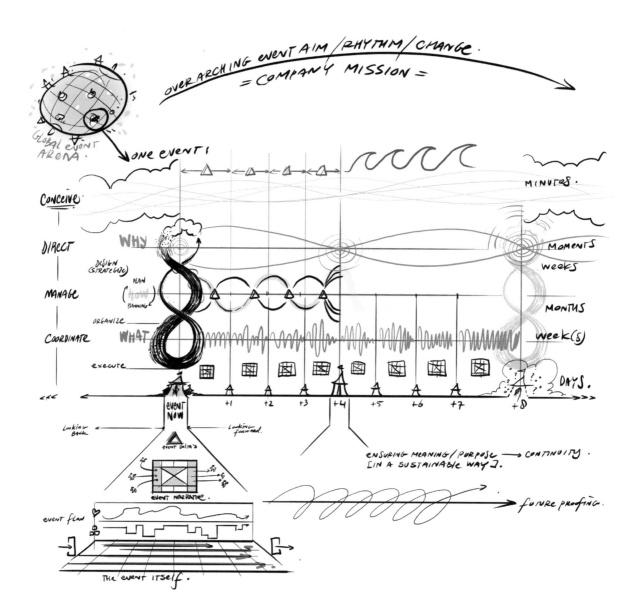

The fifteen-minute meeting the executive can spare affords no time for descriptions of the process. They are outcome thinkers: don't tell me how you do it, just do it (and do it right). This is the overview perspective.

A designer might excitedly explain process instead of results: we used this tool, and this canvas, and this technique, and waste time in the fifteen minute check-in meeting. This is the greatest pitfall of a designer failing to align perspective. Process details do not matter to the Outcome thinker. The executive loses faith and denies the resortuces necessary for productive design. Or, executives, with attention needed elsewhere, may not hear the message of what is needed by designers to arrive at the intended goal.

If these differences in perspective are not recognized, no one will be satisfied. But if executives (and owners and their gatekeepers) understand where designers are coming from, and if designers perform their process and deliver innovative outcomes, the door is open for the outcome thinker to accept the designers' process. Afterall, such meetings are events, too. They satisfy the criteria of being a gathering of two or more people with something at stake. And these events are successful when they embrace the integration of these different perspectives.

Knowing that those with closer perspectives embrace process and those observing from higher altitude perspectives embrace outcomes will allow people to understand each other. Collaborators with various perspectives dedicate time according to their altitude. Such understanding leads to engagement, communication, and the ability to have people with other perspectives see beyond their particular perch. Knowing that diverse perspectives are valid in targeting the same goal will allow for faith in each other and a sense of a shared mission. Outcomes versus process will be analysed in much greater detail in the next chapter.

3. Zoom In / Zoom Out

Zoom In/Zoom Out has already been explained in chapter one. It is important to consider again here because it affects perspective as well. Even similar stakeholders working on the same team at the same altitude—two designers, for example—can have different perspectives and end up working at cross purposes if they are unclear about how zoomed in or out to be.

It is often the case that zooming out is difficult for people. The broad view can be either too hard to define, too full of unknowns. When overwhelmed with such uncertainty, people often take refuge in managing individual details and lose sight of the bigger picture. But it is critical to zoom out early (for instance, by defining Horizons) and again from time to time in order to ensure the overarching, long-term aims are defined, that everyone is aware, and that the details still serve.

Being able to shift between scales of detail, or scope, is one skill. Being able to know when to shift zoom, how to communicate the shift, and recognize when others are in a different zoom perspective are additional skills. The application of Zoom In/Zoom Out for Perspective integration is exactly this set of skills. If you have the sense that there is misunderstanding between Perspectives, that others are not seeing what you're seeing, perhaps you can identify that they are too zoomed in and need clarification on the overall goal(s). Or they are too zoomed out and could benefit from identifying the link between specific details and the big picture.

Events are mechanisms of change, and that change can be measured by deltas of different scales, from the granular to the grand scheme of things. Using an understanding of zoom in and zoom out helps to identify misaligned perspectives and unify them.

The text in the image: VISION OF THE FUTURE, EMBEDDING KNOWLEDGE & LEARNING, THEME NEXT YEAR // DROPPING ATTENDANCE, NOW!, △⁻⁴, △⁻³, △⁻², △⁻¹, +1, +2, +3

4. When In The Timeline

Perspective is also influenced by when in the timeline a stakeholder is concentrating their attention. Because an event is planned in advance, is experienced over time, is often part of a long-term plan, and with results to be assessed afterward, there are many different moments to consider.

Series of events, and even a single event, are made up of specific deltas. This fact must first be understood by all. Then defining those deltas, their progression, and how they sequence toward a specified culmination allow collaborators to revisit them out of sequence. Altitudes, stakes, zoom are diverse, and can even be examined out of sequence, but only when everyone is looking at the same moment. Collaborators must first set up and agree to a detailed timeline and then communicate clearly with each other about when in the timeline they are focusing.

GETTING THINGS 'IN PERSPECTIVE'

These four task-specific variables of perspective—stake, altitude, zoom, and when— can be understood, identified, communicated, and adjusted. But there is something more. Integration does not guarantee that you have arrived at 'the ability to perceive things in their actual inter-relations or comparative importance' (definition 3c.). Your perspectives can still be inapplicable. Even if two people embrace the others' perspective, whether by coincidence or by having consciously shifted perspective, they may not have things 'in perspective'.

In perspective and out of perspective refer to the appropriateness of the perspective to the object at hand. Let's reconsider the sketch of the two people looking at the shape on the ground: it is one closed loop and an open hook. Mr. 6 has gone over to Ms. 9's side to understand his point of view. But what if it really is a 6? Or what if

it is actually the letter g after all? Just try playing the card game Uno with a five-year-old. They will try to play a 6 card on a 9. It takes some repeated explanation for that youngster to notice the little underline below those two numbers to see what is right. A 6 is not a 9. You have to decode the clues to know for sure.

Achieving perspective integration is only part of the process. Being in perspective as opposed to being out of perspective is the rest of the process. Being in perspective means seeing the actual relationship between objects, correctly regarded in terms of relative importance and to the whole. Being out of perspective means seeing the wrong relationships, regarding them incorrectly, or misunderstanding them relative to the whole.

Collaborators must not only understand that there are different perspectives, but also that things must be 'in perspective', that things are correctly regarded. Multiple valid perspectives does not mean that every consideration is valid. There are also incorrect and incomplete ones. In the next section we'll discuss ways of managing these concerns successfully.

How do you know whether or not your perspective is 'in perspective'? How do you know if you are not simply being insistent and narrow-minded by trying to bring others to your side of the table? How do you know if you have walked around a true 6 just to appease the mistaken Ms. 9? The answer lies in empathy and that it flows in two directions. There is a methodology to achieve reciprocal empathy, which takes us now to the Process of Perspective integration.

EVENT DESIGN
MASTERMIND

CHANET HAM, CEM - UTS, CED+

OWNER
PX EVENT GLOBAL DMC AUSTRALIA MALAYSIA

For the team to really understand the event owner's need, my skillset of facilitating the event design process has been a breakthrough. Becoming a Trusted Advisor gave me the capability to converse with the event owner about the design of pivotal moments. We both won big.

EVENT DESIGN
MASTERMIND

PATTI SPANIOLA, CMP, CED+
DIRECTOR OF CONFERENCES & EVENTS
UNIVERSITY OF WEST FLORIDA

It is all too common designers find themself in a debrief session and the event owners say things like "We didn't get the Behaviour change we were looking for," or "Did we miss an opportunity to understand and connect with other important stakeholders?". By starting and engaging teams in conversations about change early in the design process, we have had great success in maintaining that alignment throughout the life of the event.

PROCESS

The primary element in working with different perspectives is simply being aware that it is internal and an individual responsibility to be aware of different perspectives, the reasons why different perspectives exist, and that they all are valid until scrutinized, as described above.

Quite simply, the application of the ideas in this discussion is to employ it as an approach to other tools and steps in the creation of an event. You would still have an initiating conversation; claim time, team, and space being able to do that will be the focus of Chapters 5 and 6 of this book (and chapter 4 of the Event Design Handbook); define Horizons of Change; identify, analyse, and align stakeholders; make a short list of the ones to delight. But the mission now is to encourage diversity of perspective in the process rather than to create a unity of opinion. Just like it takes empathy to align stakeholders, it takes empathy to embrace diversity in your colleagues opinions.

In each tool, empathy is critical. It is how you can ensure that you are seeking truth, especially the unexpected, rather than preparing to push forward your big idea. If you have the time, review these tools.

The empathy process is the delving into the perspectives of others. You leave your own behind, at least for the

moment. They may initially find your perspective surprising, but if you have empathised with their position accurately and tailored your communication accordingly, you can engage in constructive ways. It's then possible to invite others to see the perspective you have been holding, to empathize themselves and see something grand. At the same time, it is useful to re-examine your own perspective to see how it may have changed after empathizing. After all, if the process is one of discovery, you must have gained new insights as part of your personal Delta.

Being able to shift among different perspectives and to maintain the integrity of those different perspectives means you have achieved flexible focus. It means you, yourself, can maintain multiple perspectives at different time, encourage others to feel welcome in theirs, encourage diversity in team creation, encourage others to shift perspective but feel safe in expressing their personal preferences.

The next part of the process is to combine the multitude of perspectives you have analysed. This helps you zoom out to see a wide view of the master goal, and to prepare yourself to describe to stakeholders how the design options meet their individual Needs in conjunction with the Needs of others.

OUTCOME

Becoming adept at integrating multiple perspectives will allow you to think in more creative and non-canonical ways and therefore deliver better results and more options for more people. Maybe a flat, top-down view is the best way to introduce your chair or teacup, or maybe you want to show multiple perspectives of your object like a Cubist painter.

Perspective fluidity will foster a common language which will prevent miscommunication and frustration. Instead, you will achieve a diversity of thoughts, the ability to explore those different ways of thinking, and delve into the unknown (more on this in later chapters). You will start to look at events from different angles yourself and come up with creative solutions individually, and as a team. And you will also gain clarity, even though the ideas may be unexpected. They will be more creative, more clear, more shared and invested in, and ultimately better.

Having a facilitated team of people to think very diversely to come up with the broadest possible options is the purpose. You look at those options through the lens of the behaviour you're trying to change. You select what works best. Then, you will deliver better prototypes.

Additionally, people who usually stay in their specific altitude will be able to visit other altitudes during the process, before the event proves to be the final test. For example, event owners can understand what is going on with the designers at ground level. And designers can understand the interests of the executives and their concern for the overarching aim.

The results will not only be that you have a strategy to have more fruitful conversations, but also that people with different perspectives will understand each other's tasks and requirements and trust others in the process. Without a grasp of multiple perspectives, intention can still be aligned (for example by defining Horizons together), but behaviour can still be misaligned, leading to unintended results. We want intended results. We can identify them and design for that.

The organization has an overarching aim, what the executive is trying to achieve. The journey to deliver for that aim

is supported by many pillars, varying perspectives, included, which can be culminated and navigated. Though the team is diverse, if you trust the team and trust the process, the process will prove to be coordinated and collaborative, instead of lonely. And owners will be happier.

Events are designed moments of change. The Delta of Behaviour change is the intended result of a perspective shift. Event Design is entirely a matter of perspective differences. Perspective differences over time, perspective differences between stakeholders. It's true for your own perspective and how you must step outside of it. It's true for your appreciation of and engagement with the perspectives of those you work with. And it is true for the Deltas of your event participants.

So is your pain the process or the outcome? Or is it both?

PAUL RULKENS

A MATTER OF PERSPECTIVE, A WAY OF LOOKING

CHAPTER 02

If I look at an event the two most important perspectives for me are risk and reward. If we talk about reward, reward is about how the event will improve the condition of the organization. In other words, how will it connect to achieving its strategic goals? And I would love to see events positioned as part of an entire program. So not solely an event, but part of a program to achieve something. That creates value in my eyes.

Now the other part of the coin is risk with every single initiative we take, we are exposed to risk. So my other question would be: how are you going to manage the biggest risk of the event and having your perspective there, making sure that things work out fine? That I can sleep at night. This is a very, very important consideration.

So here is the thing, whenever you talk about events and you look at that perspective, I would love to hear your connection to rewards. How would it improve my condition? But especially to risks, what is it that we're going to do to minimize exposure to things, which I don't want to see.

Take a moment to reflect. Grab a pen.
Jot down the answers to the following questions:

What recent conversation did you have (that you left to chance) that you wish you could redo?

How would you address risk and reward with your event owner in your next conversation?

What question would you ask to see it like they do?

03.
―

PROCESS
OR OUTCOME,
OR BOTH?

―――― CHAPTER 03

PROCESS
UTCOME

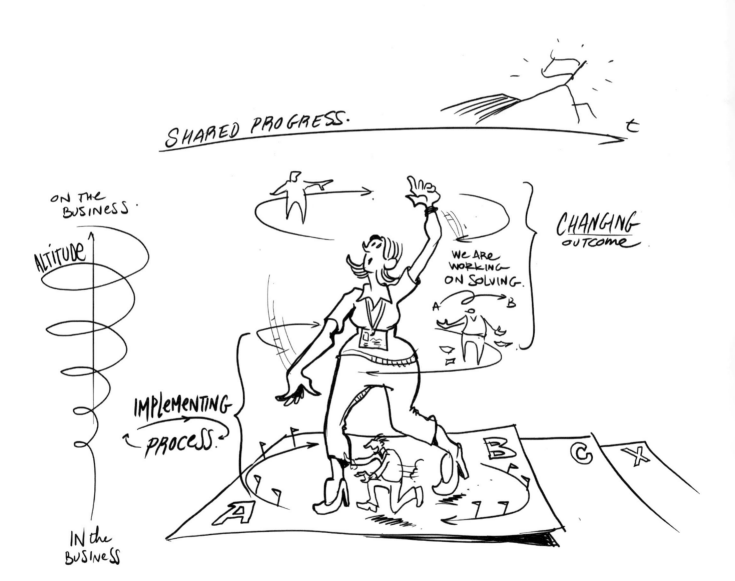

QUESTION TO ASK

The pain question for this chapter is split because we're discussing two distinct ways of thinking, how they differ, and how they can go hand in hand.

The process thinker's pain question is: **Why do they question the process?**
Whenever I make an outcome goal, I usually fail. Whenever I make a process goal, I usually succeed. But when I try to bring the process to the table, people are skeptical.

The outcome thinker's pain question is: **Why do they bother me with the how and the why?**
The outcome has been stated clearly. Fussing about it wastes time. People know what to do and yet they deliver disappointing results.

This topic's gain question covers what is really at stake, progress: How can we measure progress together?

The basic answer to this question, as you may have guessed, is the combination of two different ways of thinking. That's what this chapter is about: combining process and outcome ways of thinking. Process thinking and outcome thinking are simply two different, but equally necessary examinations of progress. They both focus on results, but go about it in different ways. Either way of thinking standing alone is incomplete, but together they can join forces and move the process forward. When process thinking and outcome thinking regard each other, we'll see how their analytical methods can fold together and produce a clear timeline and metric. But first let's distinguish between them and discern who is thinking in which manner.

PRINCIPLES

Some really enjoy process. They have a preference for taking a step-by-step approach whenever presented with a challenge. It enables them to tackle a challenge in a very systematic way which will then lead them to the outcome.

Others are really agnostic to the method of getting to the outcome and are simply interested in the final outcome, regardless of how you get there. And, even when there is an outcome without a formal process, the way the outcome is created is also a process. The question is, is it systematic?

In the Event Design Handbook we describe a systematic approach to designing innovative events using the Event Canvas.

It enables teams to get to grips with a process. It breaks down how events create value through behaviour change while getting team members on the same page. It offers a design process with linear and lateral thinking which allows facilitators to lead their teams to analyse the stakeholders who need to be delighted. It subsequently culminates in prototyping how that can best be done as designers then propose possible alternatives to reach the overarching aim, also known as the outcomes.

Most operations in organizations have a process. Keeping the books, performance reviews, distribution methods, quality control, and the like all deserve their due processes. It's even included in the phrase, hiring process. Somehow, events are still the wild west, relegated to last minute, ad hoc, duct tape sessions. It doesn't have to be.

In place of event planning, event design is the allocation of a process to treat events with a similar professional mindset. The aspirations people have for their events demand as much.

Furthermore, practicing the process of event design will solve the problems stated above for the planner or owner because it produces results that are thought through by a team, measurable, repeatable, and scalable. For the occasional event designer, the design process will define the design goal and behaviour change for each of the stakeholders. And for the outcome seeker, it will provide options, insight, and more satisfied stakeholders.

Events deserve a design process. Process requires time, team, and space. The stepped approach by a team requires the event owner to trust the team and trust the process. It requires patience from the event owner to suspend their disbelief. Wanting an outcome is not the same as knowing what the outcome is going to be.

Because process and outcome are inseparable, the process has validation points along the way to get the buy-in from the outcome thinker during the process. This enables the outcome thinker to monitor the progress and ensures them that the design team is on track.

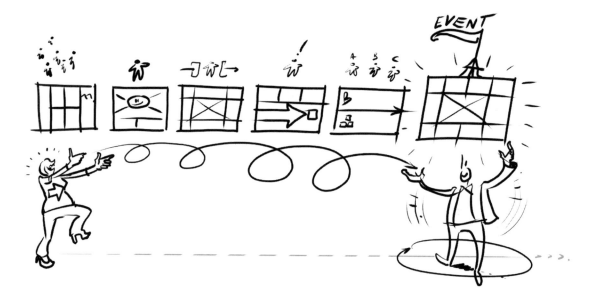

The design team adopts a "yes, and" mindset (instead of a "yes, but" one) which builds momentum for the best possible prototypes to be presented to the outcome thinker. The outcome thinker then has the choice of multiple options and can make a decision based on the design team's recommendations.

The benefit of combining process with outcome includes that it :
- Is based on stakeholder needs
- Involves a diverse set of team member's views
- Provides thought clarity for the team
- Dispels the negative impacts of groupthink
- Can be validated along the way
- Creates more predictability towards the desired outcome
- Results are visible and logical
- Is scalable
- Is repeatable
- Is iterative
- Gets everyone on the same page

In this chapter we delve into how these two ways of thinking go hand-in-hand. In order to obtain the best results, it should be considered to be process and outcome. They work in tandem.

The communication between the perspectives is a two-way street, or maybe better yet, a constructive feedback loop. Each way of thinking can define its overarching aim and expectations, give the other side the space they need to develop and define those goals and expectations, deliver something workable for the other in regard to the expectations, and to check in on each other at regular intervals.

The outcome thinker develops and delivers the ultimate horizon to the designers who simultaneously deliver a road map for their design process. Both parties understand the goal, the timeline, and the process and can communicate with each other about progress. In a timely manner, the design team delivers a selection of paths to reach the horizon and the executive selects one and sets it into motion.

In later chapters we will discuss how to claim time for the design process. In this chapter we explore how combining process thinking with outcome thinking is key to delivering tangible results. How it allows a diverse team to apply design thinking, and that it is a methodology for zeroing in on the best, and often unexpected prototypes.

What we're looking at in this chapter is the ability for a team to dig into a challenge, progress through the steps to identify multiple ways to tackle the challenge and then be able to measure the results of the outcome versus the original expectation. Progress and results: those are two different things, yet they are intertwined.

A NOTE ABOUT WORDING

We will examine two parallel concerns about production with the words process and outcome, but these are also words we use in each chapter to create four sections: question to ask/ problem to solve, principles, process, and outcomes. Those section headings stand as a repeating outline to frame one concern at a time. Process and outcome as section headings are general and do not mean the same thing as the topic of this chapter.

Or do they? The section of each chapter called question/ problem establishes a concern. The section, principles, defines the background of the way the world works in regard to such a concern. Together these two describe pre-existing parameters. In the chapter structure, the following two sections are a guide to what may be. The process section introduces methodologies to enact in order to innovate and the outcome section suggests the results you can expect.

VINCENT ROUX, CED, MBA
DIRECTOR
EVENT DESIGN COLLECTIVE FRANCE

Change can be unpredictable and unexpected. Designers need to be able to have a conversation about change and the process of designing for it. Together they can articulate and determine the required behaviour change. These conversations help to achieve the most important objectives. The conversation is a must have!

STEFANIE SIMMONS, CMM, DES, CTA, CED+
PRINCIPAL CONSULTANT
ONEEDGE

The key is in the learning and implementation of Design to Change, which elevates executive-level stakeholder alignment, curiosity, and process to accelerate the speed of having "meaningful conversations". It is in the strategic conversations of collaboration with conscious event design, that transforms an event story through value creation modeled in Behaviour outcomes journey. The intention to believe in bigger insights through clarity, commitment, and consistency influences impact on event experiences.

PROCESS

In order to avoid process and outcome confusion we have to establish that there are distinct differences. Each has their own preferred language to define what is what. It is important to respect those differences. The Event Owner wants outcomes. The Event Designer needs time for their process.

It is best to visualise that over time and be consciously aware that process comes before outcomes. The process supports decision making. It is not there to draw up the one conclusion already conceived by the outcome thinker. It's therefore important to be aware that many event owners may not be aware of the existence or necessity of a process.

The biggest pitfall for the event designers can be that they are so obsessed with their process that they speak

the wrong language to the event owner. The designers should not explain "how" they do it but focus on the language of the outcomes "when" they do it. It is important for the event owner to understand "what" can be expected "when" without worrying about the "how".

The designer can be held responsible for the process, not the outcome. The event owner has to be aware of the process timeline and understand that they have to make validation decisions along that timeline.

Everyone should understand going into the process how it is shaped: how innovative thinking can still be consistent and adhere to a timeline.

Now that the designers have their people, space, and time, their first objective is to define the design goals. We

will discuss this in more detail in the next chapter about Wants and Needs, but briefly, now, it is worth mentioning that this first objective is a re-defining. The event owner may have described what she wants, but the design team must come to a consensus about what she, and other stakeholders, need.

This step does three things. It creates a complete list of relevant stakeholders that need to be delighted and it articulates the behaviour change per stakeholder. The team will settle into a shared language, remember the value of change, and focus on entry and exit Behaviour. The change between these entry and exit behaviours, we call the Event Delta.

Next the designers articulate what needs to happen between entry Behaviour and exit Behaviour. This change

is the design goal, called the Event Delta. This leads to a myriad prototypes that can be chosen from and converted into desired outcomes. In the end, the design Process is completed with the prototype delivery. The outcome thinker is now responsible for what comes of it. The "Delta" marks the end of the process and the beginning of the outcome.

If the outcome thinker is aware of these steps, she can check in from time to time and see that the unrestrained elements of the design process are still in line with the ultimate goal. In the end, she has the opportunity to select the best out of proposed prototypes as recommended by the design team. And she ultimately takes responsibility for the results for the chosen prototype.

OUTCOME

The results of using outcome thinking in tandem with process thinking is that your team will be able to draw on a process to consciously design for outcomes. Teams will be on the same page, working on one common event narrative. They will be clear about the timing and usefulness of two different perspectives. The process will be ordered, sequential, and demonstrate causality in the delivered designs.

Understanding the difference between and the symbiosis of process and outcome will make teams more successful in understanding each other: effective in addressing change, fine tuned to the listener, able to adapt the message to process and outcome thinkers.

Additionally, the team will be able to ask and answer several critical questions. How big is the change we are willing to attempt? If we are to create ripples in the pond, are we throwing a pebble or are we throwing in a large rock? Are we ready as an organization for the results of that change? Are we prepared to create that change? Who acts when? How many incremental steps does it take?

By initiating the design of an event with such a conversation about the current state, the desired future state, and the arc of change, the collaborators reach an alignment with each other about the overarching aim and can develop an understanding of the language for outcomes and obtain appreciation for the language of process.

Being specific about the resources needed and the sequence of the process is essential. For example, you could spend eight total hours over two days; six hours to spend on analyzing the stakeholders, their wants and needs, and their deltas; one and a half hours for generating prototypes; and a half hour to debrief the executive. This forces the designers to take responsibility and assures the executive that there is in fact a methodology and that someone is facilitating it.

Being clear on this requires people to listen for the sake of understanding rather than listening to respond. In this way, rapport is formed and relationships will be built on trust. Design can be the bedrock of that very trust.

That trust carries through the process. Executives maintain a proud sense of sponsorship and ownership during the process. And by having this permission followed through, designers can maintain a continuity of meaning and purpose.

With such trust and partnership, events will turn into time well invested, be more interesting and chosen as a preferred mechanism to deliver change over time.

Process thinking or outcome thinking standing alone are incomplete, but when they join forces they will move the organisation forward to create shared progress in the desired direction of change.

PAUL RULKENS

PROCESS OR OUTCOME, OR BOTH?

CHAPTER 03

The three most important questions that I would like to have answered are the following: One, what does success of the event look like? Number two, how do we know we are successful? And number three, how will success of the event help me to achieve my strategic goals.

This for me captures the essence of the outcome I want to achieve. Now, when it comes to process, there's something I need to know as well, which is: the implicit and explicit boundaries. In other words, if we want to achieve those outcomes, regardless of what happens, these are the boundaries we need to stay within.

For example, we need to stay within budget. We need to stay within audience participation. We need to connect with other initiatives in the organization. And as an executive, this perspective is very important. If I could define the outcome. And if I can define the boundary conditions in which we can achieve the outcome, then the process itself for me, is free to do whatever is necessary in order to make it happen.

The biggest mistake is people who focus on process instead of focus on outcome.

Take a moment to reflect. Grab a pen.
Jot down the answers to the following questions:

What question will you ask to define what success looks like for the event, and how it will help the event owner achieve their strategic goals?

What questions do you need to ask to make sure outcomes are delivered upon?

How does your conversation with the event owner enable you to identify the boundaries?

How does the design process enable the desired outcome within the boundaries ?

How would you build rapport with the event owner to gain their trust and the event design process you intend to use?

04.

WANTS
VERSUS NEEDS

QUESTION TO ASK

The pain question for this chapter is: **Why do people sometimes under-appreciate my suggestions, concepts, or solutions to their problems?**

The event owner can experience renewed pain after expressing what they want, when designers sequester themselves and then return with a variety of different and unexpected solutions. Owners know what they want.

They have expressed it and directed people to work on it. Why can't they just get what they want?

Conversely, when designers convert the owner's wants into needs, the owner resists.

The gain question for this chapter is: **How do I get people to be patient for even better prototypes?**

PRINCIPLES

Your headache is persisting, and so you go to the doctor to ask for pain killing medication. It is the doctor's job to hear you out and annotate what they have heard. But the painkiller carries risks and may not solve the underlying problem. It is, therefore, also the job of the experienced expert to then compare what they hear to what they know about what works and what doesn't. It is their job to do more than just satisfy what you want. They must investigate what is really needed to solve the pain.
In a similar way, designers function as diagnosticians. Event owner wants and needs are likely to be different things, and understanding their difference is a significant part of the design process.

Wants are self-expressed, an expression of pains that are only skin-deep, and the satisfaction of wants is usually short-lived, sometimes even resolved before the event itself. 'More profit' is a want.

Needs are deeper. They describe the position of an organization within the external real world. They specify long-term aims. And they usually are discovered through investigation. 'Building trust' is a need.

For someone to commit to owning an event at all, they have already done some diagnostics of their own and determined what they want. They want something in their world to be different, to change, to improve, and they have decided an event can do that. This longing for a future state can make something lacking in the now feel like a vulnerability. And people don't like being vulnerable. They want to change their pain into a gain as soon as possible. They feel compelled to rush and are over-confident in the want they've already identified. They can be over-eager and under-prepared.

Enter the design team. When people identify what they want, it is possibly a short-term solution to a long-term pain. The principal objective of the design process is to come up with the best prototypes to long-term pains for the event owner. Designers investigate the need after hearing the want.

Event owners communicate with the term need rather than want, that 'need' might indeed be a want; 'I need an event this summer like what Red Bull did last year', is an expression of a want. Self-expressed need might actually be a want. It is worth investigating.

"I WANT IT ALL!!!"

HAVING THE DESIRE OR WISH TO POSSES OR REACH SOMETHING.

REQUIRE SOMETHING BECAUSE IT IS ESSENTIAL.

YOU NEED TO MAKE THIS STEP.

SOURCE OF MOTIVATION

Consider this. Bad habits develop from the pursuit of a short-term satisfaction of some wants (for instance a cigarette, interupting, blaming). In contrast, good habits evolve from investigating the long-lasting benefits of addressing needs. This does not mean that all Wants are inherently destructive. They're informative at least, and can sometimes truly be needs. A person with a headache wanting a glass of water might actually need a glass of water. The good news is that either the wants are complete, and if not, the needs can be distilled from the mash of wants. From their want, you can come to understand their pain, their need, and determine the action to take.

The conversation about diagnosis and remedy can be uncomfortable, though. No one likes to be questioned about or told to wait for what they want. It is in our instinct to please others, especially when there is a hierarchy. You tell me you want a certain result. And I am tempted to respond, 'Of course. On it.' But that often produces disappointing results, which in turn leads to an uncomfortable review conversation. Having the conversation about needs is uncomfortable, too, but not as uncomfortable as an unsuccessful event. To deliver stronger prototypes, designers must apply a process to investigate needs. How do you make that constructive conversation less uncomfortable? By having a structured process to investigate needs.

101

EVENT DESIGN
MASTERMIND

ANDREA VERNENGO, CED
DIRECTOR
EVENT DESIGN COLLECTIVE ITALY

Every so often you end a conversation with a buyer, and you feel successful as you have received the great opportunity to send a proposal.

Then all at once you realise that you are only executing his wants but have not dug into his needs!

Never leave a conversation without having clarified needs against wants, and drive the conversation to make sure you are covered before agreeing on any next steps or on sending a proposal.

GERRIT JESSEN, CMP CMM CED

DIRECTOR
EVENT DESIGN COLLECTIVE GERMANY

I've discovered that if you are equipped with the powers to explore the problem, you can make a real difference. Amping up the pain gently by asking why questions, allows you to contribute your superpowers when the stakes are high.

PROCESS

Designers are facilitators. It begins with an initiating conversation when outcomes are first being requested and before there is permission to design. The event owner has an idea, a want. This presents a necessary and healthy imbalance. The owner comes with a determination. The designers do not. They should be free of any preconceived notions of their own. It interferes with truly hearing the pains the owner is trying to resolve. The initiating conversation is for listening and understanding. And yet, it is also a conversation for the designer to reply with specifics, not about the owner's idea itself, but about the process to come.

Once a designer explains the how of process, she can defend the why of it. The designer should explain that experience has shown that there is a value gap between designing for wants, which is what we're discussing now, and designing for needs, which has to be investigated. There is a proven process for doing this efficiently. Don't worry, the wants we're learning about now will in no way be dismissed or ignored. The results will be designed to solve problems embedded in the want, but that requires digging deeper into undiscovered needs and satisfying those. Be aware, some identification of needs may be unexpected, but they will be addressed in the process.

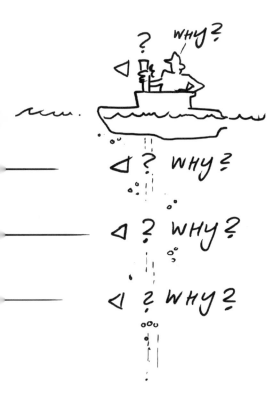

Here is an example of a sequence of questions you could ask:
1. "How did you realize this is what you want?"
2. "Is there a problem you can identify that you are trying to solve?"
3. "Though the event is going to be planned for next season, where do you want to be three years from now?"

First, the designer requests permission to ask questions. This request reassures executives that the designer is not pressing a preconceived agenda, interrogating or criticizing, but rather listening and understanding the interests of the owner in exactly the way explained earlier: to uncover the pain embedded in the want that has led to the conversation in the first place. A good first question to ask, once the c vpermission to do so has been granted, is, "How did you realize this is what you want?" Or perhaps, "Is there a problem you can identify that you are trying to solve?" "Though the event is going to be planned for next season, where do you want to be three years from now?" Such questions provoke the owner to recognize that investigative questioning can fill in what have been blind spots,

to do some investigating themselves, and to understand that the designers are taking their role as a trusted advisor seriously.

It is also useful to ask "Why" questions, especially to understand better any details that are described as Wants that seem particularly specific. Why exactly do you want an event like Red Bull? This reminds everyone that there is something of value within that want. Later, once it is examined in the design process, that detail of value can lead to a more complete event narrative. But without asking why, the design team can't build value to satisfy needs. Satisfying a Want just leads to knockoff Red Bull events as requested.

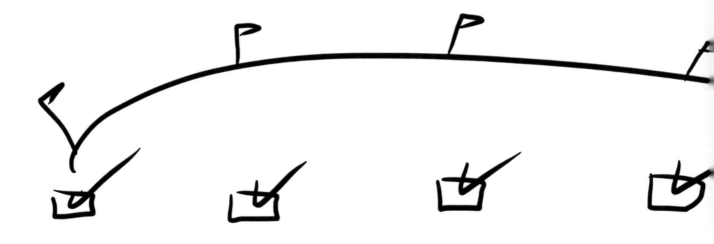

Beware, blurting out "Why?" to every "Want" can come across as overly inquisitive. The point is to understand, and so the why question has a partner: an understanding check-in. Before asking a Why question, repeat what it is you understood from the last statement. This reassures your conversation partner that you are listening closely and striving to understand completely. It also will work to delineate what you have accurately understood and what, in fact, you have not. If your brief reiteration is off the mark, the other speaker can clarify and advance your understanding before you ask the Why question. But, if your recap is accurate, the follow-up Why question comes from a stance of alignment, and merely asks for more depth. It makes people reflect about deeper significance and more lasting value.

This conversation is the first pivotal moment. Be prepared for more pivotal moments along the way. Pivotal moments are when coordination is tested and corrected if necessary. It is between the pivotal moments when designers have the freedom to create, design, and even fail without having to own it. But the pivotal moments are when things are decided and agreed to. The process itself is a cascade of pivotal moments: setting the overarching aim, analyzing each stakeholder in their own time (including Wants versus Needs), prototyping, delivering.

The event itself is a pivotal moment, the enactment of the design and the delta. A review conversation after the event to evaluate the design is another critical moment. And throughout the process there should be brief informal check-ins between designers and owners, which will be pivotal.

But the pivotal moment of delivering prototypes can be particularly unnerving for both designers and owners. Having been given the permission to design and having enjoyed the creative process, designers now have to convince others that their innovative prototypes are practical and serve the overarching aim of satisfying the owner's needs. It is only natural designers hope that people will be impressed, and consequently fret about rejection. The burden for the event owners is that they are ultimately responsible for outcomes, but are being presented with multiple, and unexpected, prototypes. They have to process the design team's new ideas and also have to choose. This can be a delicate moment.

The responsibility of the designer is finished at delivery, but the responsibility of the executive is only half complete and she has just been presented with a new turn of affairs. There are a few tactics for alleviating these pains. One is to have an initiating conversation that explains the process and the greater value of addressing Needs. Another is for periodic validation points and check-ins to maintain understanding. And the final one is for the design team to enter the delivery conversation with a full accounting of the results of their process, not a description of the process itself, but how their analysis of each of the stakeholders' needs solve the fundamental challenge of the event owner.

INCREMENTAL

OUTCOME

In the course of the initiating conversation, people approaching the creation of an event from different perspectives agree to a process and its timeline, find a common language about methodology as opposed to results, and actually begin the shift from wants to needs. This preliminary step for the shift can happen in the first conversation with questions from the designer. Then, having been permitted to set themselves in the right direction, designers can generate more appropriate prototypes.

But more, they can take the pulse of an organization. By understanding the difference between wants and needs, that needs are embedded within wants, and that needs represent the real problem to solve, designers and executives together can embrace the design process. They are not simply entering a design process for an event, but designing incremental change steps over time towards the overarching aim of that organisation.

108   WANTS VERSUS NEEDS

PAUL RULKENS

WANTS VERSUS NEEDS

CHAPTER 04

What I value as an executive is having a trusted advisor. I may not know much about event design and that's why I need help.

What I expect from a trusted advisor is that he or she shifts my thinking from what I want, because I know what I want, to what I need. That's the value distance where the trusted advisor can truly add value to the conversation.

So once you tell me what I need and I concur, the second step is give me some freedom in order to get there. And giving me freedom means that it's not only important to tell me what I need, but it's also important to give me options to get there. And once I'm capable of choosing between options I have the feeling that I am in control, but also leaving important stuff to my trusted advisor when it comes to event design. And that's the core of being successful, a balance between giving me what I need and at the same time, giving me options, how to get there.

Take a moment to reflect. Grab a pen.
Jot down the answers to the following questions:

When was the last time you identified a gap between the want and the need?

What check in questions will you ask to verify understanding?

Take A Moment ... REFLECT.

What questions will you ask to help you identify the value distance to uncover the real need in a next conversation?

Without giving the solutions, how will you manage the expectation of giving options at a later time?

05. —

SESSION DAY!
EMBRACE THE CHAOS!
PROCESS DESIGN

PUTTING DESIGN ON THE AGENDA

THE AG

QUESTION TO ASK

In the previous chapters we discussed different considerations for collaborating with a diverse team: defining the Horizon of Change, embracing multiple Perspectives, combining Process Thinking with Outcome Thinking, and finding Needs within Wants. In this chapter we will bring all of those tools together in describing the Design Process itself and how it creates value.

If you already find the design process useful, you may have asked yourself the pain question to ask for this chapter: **Why do some people not trust design?**

Or you want to know: **How can we get design on the agenda?**

The answers will be explored in more detail in the following sections, but here, the brief answer is that entering the design process can feel like opening a can of worms. You don't know what you'll find in there, everything looks like a mess, and it's hard to tell one thing from another. Design can appear to some as chaos and people find it hard to invest faith in chaos. It makes people wonder.

Wonder implies doubt. Ambiguity is the source of doubt. You can't design without doubt. Combine these elements and design becomes evident.

It requires trust to manage such wriggling unknowns: trust in the team; trust in a methodology, that such a structured method provides lifelines out of the chaos; trust that a dynamic design process, rather than linear "problem-solution"-thinking, actually solves more problems; trust that problem is not a bad word. We use the word trust here because it requires people to go into the unknown--to try things they are not used to. That creates discomfort and the instinct is to avoid it if possible. Why open up the can of worms in the first place?

Why invite chaos? It's a reasonable concern. The truth is that the chaos is out there anyway, but it can be managed only after it is identified, and then it is not chaos anymore. Better yet, the uncomfortable unknown is where you find the most innovative ideas. You can't catch the big fish if you don't become comfortable with worms. The way to get design on the agenda is to understand and explain how it structures chaos.

PRINCIPLES

Let's start by backing away from such an alarming term as *chaos*. What we're really talking about is the word problem, and there are two different ways to understand that word.

One way to use the word problem is to describe a crisis or emergency when things have gone so wrong that you encounter chaos. The other way to use the word problem is to describe uncertainty, but an uncertainty that can be solved. A math problem implies that it can be solved. All you have to do is apply the right formula, go through the steps, check your progress along the way, and you will arrive at a solution that was previously unknown. However, that uncertainty, using the word *problem* in the pursuit of a design problem, can sound to others like the emergency use of the word and the implication of chaos.

Problem in the first sense gets more attention. Crises are discovered and (hopefully) managed after the fact. When an event fails, this is a real problem. Something went wrong. What went wrong? When did it go wrong? Who's responsible for this mess? These are all retrospective investigations into the crisis kind of problem. It's not a good place to be.

The second sense of the word problem, the one that implies a solution, is prospective. It is deliberative in order to find a solution ahead of time so that there shall be no emergencies in the end. It means that at the beginning you don't shy away from chaos, because it is not chaos if you tame it. Understanding that it is simply the unknown allows you to do just that. Embracing the unknown recognizes patterns, which leads to insights and the development and adoption of appropriately designed tools. Preventive medicine is a

lot cheaper and more pleasant than treatment in a hospital bed. When we use the word problem from now on, we will mean the healthy, prospective version of the term, one that takes a realistic view on those things that you are there to solve.

Consider the squiggle diagram. The biggest tangle of lines on the left, that's the undirected and conflicting range of possibilities, the can of worms. Over time (moving towards the right in the diagram) and with a structured process, that tangle becomes a single, clear, straight strand: the event story.

The squiggle represents the first iteration of the design challenge, and the straight line leads to the final event story. It is not a simple straight line from problem to solution. From the fuzzy front end to the final prototype, a design process explores the problem to then design prototypes.

The fuzzy front end (the initial event owner's want that has not yet been fully explored) represents unknowns, unanswered questions. "But we already know what we need to know, so why muck with all that uncertainty? Close the can of worms." This is linear thinking. Linear not just that it indicates the straight line, or solution, portion of the visual, but that it goes from A to Z, from inception to solution, in a direct manner that skips over the problem identification and solving steps. Problem-solution thinking neglects the unknown, neglects the value of exploring the problem. Let's pretend there never has been a can of worms, anyway.

Design thinking allows the team to embrace a problem and explore it from multiple angles. Only then can they define the restrictions and possible ways out of it. It first recognizes that the sketch of an initial idea is an incomplete picture. It opens the door to the fact that there are unanswered questions (which is potentially unnerving), and then it finds the way out of the squiggle to the straight line. Skipping over that spaghetti doesn't mean it never existed. You can find that out retrospectively, or prospectively. Design is specifically prospective, and it is problem-centric. They enter the Event Design Black Box.

That doesn't mean that it is open ended

It does so by first opening the can of worms, and that's the hard part. People who are not familiar with the tools have to trust that there are proven methodologies, and that they are not simply unleashing chaos into their world.

Opening the can of worms and embracing the problem is a leap of faith. It raises questions and ideas that are at first contradictory or out of perspective. Finding the innovative solutions requires the process to have its time. This is an investment and requires trust in the time, tools, and team so that people can probe the problem from different angles. There is an initial shock to opening the can of worms, but there is methodology that quickly quells that shock and pays dividends.

Trust in the team also acknowledges another asset, that the process is user-centric. Design is influenced by the people doing the designing. Two different design teams will come up with different solutions. This people-based variable is quite necessary and productive. It reveals that the problem-solving process is fluid and responsive, unpredictable, unexpected--innovative. If everyone delivers the same solution, it's probably been done thousands of times before. This fluidity may be difficult to accept for people who are expecting a "correct" result rather than an effective process. But the results of an effective process are useful because they are unique. Long ago, facing similar problems, one designer invented the fork, another invented chopsticks. These are two different innovations.

Design is a process driven by people. If employed correctly, the systematic approach allows people to stay on task while exploring a variety of factors and solutions. And as those factors change over time, the team can respond. It is even important to shake up a winning team, to build new teams with new thinkers so the iterative process can remain innovative. This still requires selecting the right team and having a facilitator within that team that can guide the process through the tools and keep the team members who are new to the process clear on what task is at hand. Saying yes to design and approving a design team to go through the methodology requires a lot of trust and a lot of responsibility. So, what are the tools and systematic methods that make doing so not just a safe bet, but a wise investment?

EVENT DESIGN
MASTERMIND

ANTHONY VADE, CED+

DIRECTOR
EVENT DESIGN COLLECTIVE NORTH AMERICA

You need to be brave to lead change. Not only because the act of leading change is hard, but also because others may see you as a rebel fighting against the status quo. A leader of change must be brave, but also constantly adapt to understand the emotional impact of their most immediate conversations. Then tailor future engagement and conversations to make the change progressively more accessible to all involved.

LUCA VERNENGO, CED MEM CME-IT
DIRECTOR
EVENT DESIGN COLLECTIVE ITALY

Let's face it, change, though inevitable is sometimes scary. Learning to understand the value of change and that good change can be designed for, will enable you to put design on the agenda. The first step to start a constructive conversation.

PROCESS

The first step to putting design on the agenda is to take the leap of faith, to embrace the unanswered questions. The first person to test a parachute or sail over the horizon surely had to face serious doubts. No journey is without risks. The risk comes from the unknown, but it is the unknown that leads to innovation. The creative process is stimulated when people face the unknown, and it makes the design process rich and fun. Disbelief, thinking that something risky will not work, freezes innovation and forces people into a defensive stance against anything new, trying to avoid mistakes. The first leap is the scariest, but even then, there are lifelines in the process to keep the mission on track.

One lifeline is that time is given to stop and think, to practice design thinking instead of only problem solving, to identify problems and spend time on them in advance. This requires suspension of disbelief of everyone involved in the design team. Others include what has been covered in previous chapters. Design is when and where the tools of horizons, perspectives, process and outcome thinking, wants and needs all meet.

Defining a horizon of change allows everyone to know what the overarching aim is in terms of stakeholder Behaviour. Identifying perspectives allows for stronger communication in the creative team and greater empathy toward stakeholders. Honoring both outcome thinking and process thinking allows for the best talents of individuals to be both innovative and responsible. And weighing wants and needs also generates empathy for stakeholders, but also reminds all involved that there are not just the two actors of the event owner and the event designer, but that there are multiple stakeholders. All of these tools come together in the Event Canvas ™ methodology.

Examining graphics and information surrounding the squiggle diagram, it is clear that the timeline of reducing the chaos of the initial sketch into a gentle wave and then into a single clean straight line of an idea is guided by the systematic process of the event canvas. This is described in detail in the Event Design Handbook with fourteen specific elements. The design team addresses them systematically in three steps: First articulate the desired change based on the stakeholder needs; Then examine the design restrictions in the design frame; Next create prototypes along with the event narrative. These design outcomes can then be presented to select the final prototype. After which the event can be produced.

OUTCOME

By taking these steps, and not just skipping to the final step of producing an event based on the first rough sketch, you will produce more effective events; reduce risk in the results; find a structured method that can be applied at any time, looking forward and looking back, allowing you to create and analyze patterns in your history. You can design for change, and create a team that is user-centric, meaning they are sensitive to context, fluid, and responsive to change.

By embracing ambiguity, you run the risk of being innovative, creative, and dynamic. It's fun and rewarding. And it gets easier. You learn by doing. The second leap of faith is less scary than the first because you know that squiggle is where the good stuff comes from, and you always have within reach the lifelines of the methodology (which also become second nature).

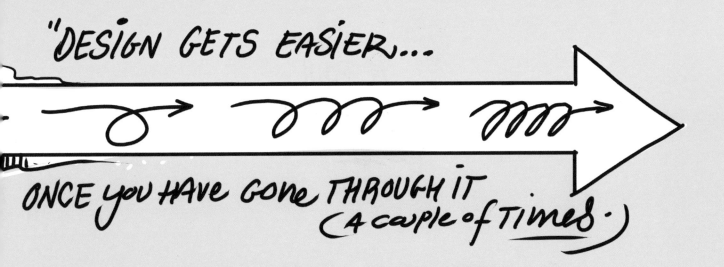

"DESIGN GETS EASIER....

ONCE YOU HAVE GONE THROUGH IT
(A couple of times.)

Design is a structured approach to consider all the tools mentioned in the previous chapters and our companion book to ensure better alignment, better and more diverse multifaceted ideas, better unexpected prototypes, a system to test results, and a system that is itself measurable, repeatable, and scalable. It simply makes for better business. And it is plannable in that you can understand what is needed as resources to claim, and predictable in that you know what to expect. Once you put design on the agenda the first time, you will find that you are excited to do it again, and that excitement spreads. This makes it easier to embed it into the organisation as a standard practice.

PAUL RULKENS

PUTTING DESIGN ON THE AGENDA

CHAPTER 05

If you want to put design on the agenda, there are two things you need to consider. The first one is ambiguity. In other words, you need to jump into the mouth of the tiger. The design process might be clear, but the outcomes and the way forward, can be somewhat unclear.

What is important for me is that, before we jump into the mouth of the tiger, we set clear boundaries for the process. In other words, dear design team, you've got all the freedom to do whatever it takes, provided that, and those are the guardrails. And once we're clear about the guardrails, then I have the feeling I'm in control and which is important for me to trust the process of putting design on the agenda.

The second element, which is important for me is if we do design in the organizations, how can we leverage what we are doing? In other words, if this process is very successful, where else can I use it in my organization to create even more value?
This is how we bring best practices to other parts of the organization. And that's a very valuable part for someone who drives the design. Where else can I use it in my organization to achieve my strategic goals?

Take a moment to reflect. Grab a pen.
Jot down the answers to the following questions:

How can you comfort your event owner that not having clarity with the initial 'ask' is ok?

What guardrails do you offer to allow the event owner to feel comfortable to say "yes" to you for event design?

How will you sketch the outcomes of event design and involve the event owner in the way forward?

How does getting design on the agenda help the event owner in other parts of the organization to achieve strategic goals?

06.

HOW TO BECOME SUCCESSFUL AT CLAIMING TIME

CHAPTER 06

133

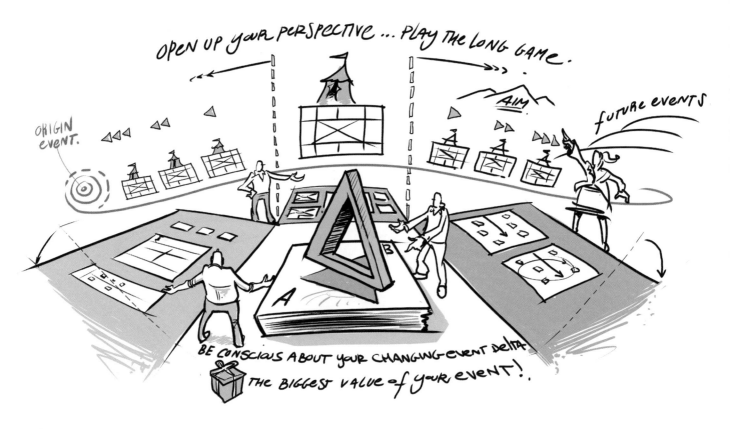

QUESTIONS TO ASK

You have succeeded in getting a design process on the agenda, or at least permission to design. But how seriously are others taking the design process? How are they backing it up with resources to support it?

The pain question in becoming successful at claiming time is: **Why are people not taking the process seriously?**

The corresponding gain question is: **How do I get people to take the long view?**

There are different levels of commitment. Perhaps design is on the agenda begrudgingly. Designers have permission to perform their routine, and that's about it.

Executives think, staff giving some thought to design is nice. It may mitigate risk, but it is not perceived as strategically critical. It is not an embedded practice.

Or perhaps you are in a situation where there is a bit more commitment behind design on the agenda.

The organizational understanding is that design could be tactically relevant and may create value in unexpected ways. It is a tool in the back of the shed to dig out from time to time when there is a clear event goal. The design process is assigned a team and some time.

Ideally, and this seems to happen within design-minded organisations, design becomes part of the culture. It is recognized to be strategically critical to organizational

success and is provided for with multiple resources as a continuing practice whether there is an imminent event or not. Recognizing and capitalizing on opportunities is an ongoing process and event design is the method of choice.

How does an organization progress from casual, permissive design to the strategic implementation of design as the defacto methodology? The answer is in the embrace of two elusive variables: in the curiosity to explore the "Why" and the "How" of the challenge and the time it requires to do so. And these are embodied in a step designers can take. The ability to claim the right resources.

PRINCIPLES

The design process requires the resources of time, team, and space. They need to be claimed first. Claiming the time to perform the task of designing is challenging. People expect answers right now.

How do you ask for time? When is the right time to approach someone with that request? How do you resist the temptation to provide immediate solutions? What is needed at the beginning of the process is not answers, but questions. It is the job of the designer to ask, and to provoke event owners by asking the right questions. The best leaders ask questions and are curious to investigate alternative options.

There is a window of opportunity to initiate questions, when an event owner first declares to want an event. Then it's time for the designer to make the claim for time, team, and space.

Also, there are layers to the hierarchy of event ownership that affect the way these conversations can be held. Some people are gatekeepers who are there to protect the event owner from uncertainty. Their job is to maintain status quo. But they are not the only people a designer can talk to.

An actual owner of an event can say yes or no to a request for design time and design ideas, and may even become enthusiastic and say yes too easily. It is why they have gatekeepers. Gatekeepers are those that can say "No" but cannot say "Yes". Approach different people at different levels in the hierarchy according to their perspective; know their interest and mandate to say "Yes". Make it clear to the person standing in the way of a "yes" to your process whether they are making a well-informed decision. If the "No" is arbitrary or ill-informed, the designer offers ways to make better decisions.

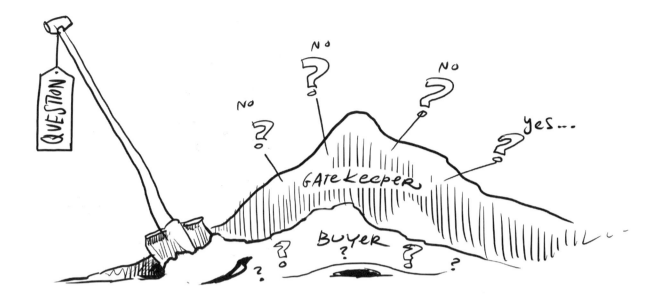

To be able to do so, the designer really only has one ask: should we take the time to explore the event owner challenge and then design for it? He explores the challenge with a team of people holding multiple perspectives to come up with prototypes that best satisfy the various stakeholders to delight. This respects the challenge more than pretending to have an answer does. The challenge has to be explored for there to be a worthy solution. And this is design. And the simple ask in the initiating conversation is time to design.

There are a handful of answers the claim might receive. A flat out no, not interested. A no with an explanation: there's not enough time, money, need, faith. There's an uninformed yes, and there's an informed yes.

An informed yes is the preferred answer, one where everyone knows the process, trusts it, believes it is in good hands, and is worth the investment. An uninformed yes is a problem, though. When someone signs off on a process, just to not have to deal with it themselves, they have not accounted for what it can deliver, and what it requires. A flat out no, well there's not much you can do about that. But a conditional no is not as bad as it might at first seem. Resistance can be converted into possibility.

When someone objects, it indicates they are interested and see potential value, but also an obstacle. The recognition of an obstacle implies the person who objects sees a path—a path obstructed, perhaps, but a path nonetheless. They see the beginning and the end, but not the journey. In other words, this is where we are now (existing situation), and this is where we would like to be (desired situation). They are attentive to conditions and willing to continue the conversation about them, but do not yet see solutions. We'll get into how to handle the conditional "no" roadblocks in the online resources. For now, we'll focus on how to ask for resources in the first place.

PROCESS

When you are faced with a challenge, you don't seek answers, you embrace the unknown and seek the right questions. But before there can be answers there has to be a time for questions. To claim time, and other resources, for design, asking questions is the key. Resist the temptation to have immediate answers. Embrace the process of considering. And encourage others to do so as well by claiming time. It turns out, designers can also use questions to do just that.

One of the strongest tactics is to question readiness. In the initiating conversation, people should ask and understand the level of readiness.

Readiness questions:

- How big is the change we want to achieve?
- Do we want to throw a pebble into the pond, or do we want to throw a boulder?
- What will be the ripple effects of such an action?
- How far will the ripple effect reach?
- Who is affected?
- How long will it last?
- If we want to throw the big stone, who and how many will lift, carry, and throw that weight and hit the mark?
- How much planning and how many tools does it take to figure out how to move a boulder and ready the far shores for the big wave to come?
- How many people, how many hours of their time, does it take to throw a pebble?

Rensis Likert, an American psychologist, devised something deceptively simple: a rating scale. It is used to quantify opinions. The Likert scale appears in surveys about the service provided by an airline and the confidence you have in a political candidate. It presents a statement and then asks you to agree or disagree on a five-point scale, ranging from strongly disagree to strongly agree. This tool is useful in identifying alignment, and exposing misalignment in countless environments.

When it comes to aligning event creators, there are several effective prompts to evaluate readiness based on some sample statements assessed on a Likert scale.

These prompts can be presented by a prepared designer or design team and will make clear what is necessary to address the problem. There needs to be a design process. There needs to be a design team (we have found that between 5 and 8 people works best; 7 is ideal). The team needs to be diverse. There needs to be time to explore the problem. There needs to be a dedicated space to design in. Once these conditions are met, your event owner should be ready to commit.

If there still remains resistance, then maybe the organisation is truly not ready for change. Saying so is a useful summation of the readiness question: Maybe we really aren't ready. If that's true, it's best to acknowledge it before you waste resources. But people most often respond to being "not ready" by examining what has made them so and seek ways to become ready.

It is incumbent on designers to be ready as well, not just with the readiness questions, but with examples and stories. To assure the executive being asked readiness questions and facing the request to delve into the unknown, announce that there is in fact a proven method to exploring the challenge that we, too, can apply to deliver better prototypes. And we know how to do it. It has proven to have been useful by others. These companies (Google, Apple, IBM, etc.) now make design process thinking a part of their core. The designer presenting himself as ready for the task builds confidence in the executive being asked to permit time and personnel for design.

To aid this conversation about readiness, the claim of the 1% "Event Design Time" calculation (as explained in the Event Design Handbook, Chapter 4) is very effective. In the conversation when the design team asks for time, it is useful to quantify the total event time. It will be a 3 hour event and there are going to be 100 people. That's 300 person-hours of "Total Event Time". Because time is the most precious commodity, we don't want to waste a minute of anyone's time. Wouldn't it be wise if we spend 1% of that time now to make sure we design it right? For a 300 person-hour event, that's 3 hours of total event design. Who can say no to that? The executive's pain to grant those resources is suddenly revealed to be so much less than the pain of a failure of that event.

READINESS PROMPTS

I am ready to evaluate my readiness

Strongly Disagree	*Disagree*	*Neutral*	*Agree*	*Strongly Agree*
◯	◯	◯	◯	●

We quantify the amount of time to spend on innovation

◯——————◯——————◯——————◯——————◯

We have a proven process to design for behaviour change innovation

◯——————◯——————◯——————◯——————◯

We can predict the outcomes of the change we design to deliver

◯——————◯——————◯——————◯——————◯

The stakes of what this change means for our organisation are business critical

◯——————◯——————◯——————◯——————◯

Our horizon of change and how we design for it to happen stretches over multiple years

◯——————◯——————◯——————◯——————◯

We have all the necessary information to make the critical decisions

◯——————◯——————◯——————◯——————◯

The magnitude of change for this initiative means this responsibility for the decision rests at the executive level

◯——————◯——————◯——————◯——————◯

OUTCOME

By engaging in the initiating meeting with questions, exploring the readiness of the organization for amplitude, magnitude, reach, and duration of consequences, and by presenting their own readiness to launch a proven, effective and time saving method, designers aim to achieve the permission to design and gain the resources of team, time, and space.

To build a team of the right size and diversity, refer to chapter 7 in the Event Design Handbook and chapter 2 in this book. A successful outcome in claiming time will be that the team can go through the design process. Refer to chapter 4 in the Event Design Handbook. A successful outcome in claiming space will be that the team can explore the breadth of possibility unperturbed,

room to think together, exercise diverse perspectives, compare and contrast them, park ideas, consider, test, and reject ideas, create prototypes, and suggest to the event owner which one the team thinks will work best for this specific design challenge.

Over time, by systematically applying design, an organization can climb the rungs of the ladder of commitment to design from 'mitigate risk, but not strategically critical', to 'tactically relevant', and ultimately to 'strategically critical'.

- Event Owner's Commitment to get involved into the Event Design Process at critical decision
- 3 phases with validation points
- with a predictable timeline

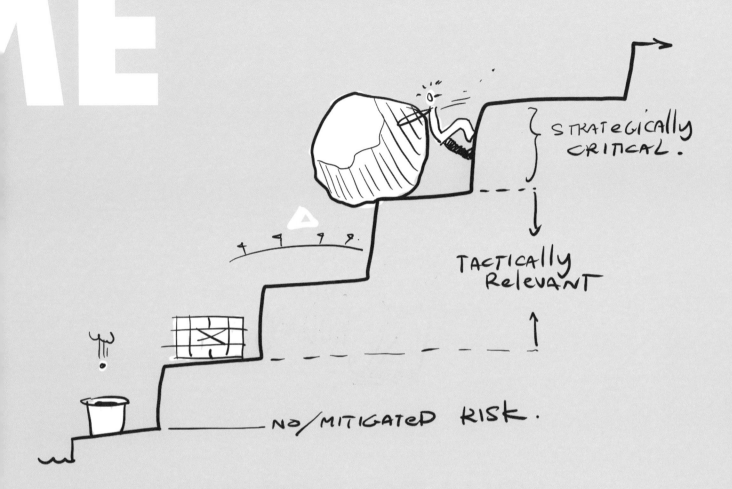

STRATEGICALLY CRITICAL.

TACTICALLY Relevant

NO/MITIGATED RISK.

At the highest level of commitment, an organization can institutionalize design as a default practice. It is good for business. Even when no event is in the works, having designers practice aspects of the process, aligning stakeholders or framing change, etc., makes it possible for organizations to understand their own past, present, and design the future. Furthermore, everyone will have information available whenever it is time to deliver an event narrative and design a selection of prototypes.

Some organisations (many notable ones, as previously mentioned) have come to recognize from their experience that providing designers with resources is business critical. For them, design is not a demand on resources. Design is the resource. The process of design is not a tool in the back of the garden shed to be retrieved only during the scramble toward an upcoming event, but the core value-driver in itself. If such a design practice can be launched and then embedded in organisations, it will be successful in delivering on their purpose.

143

PAUL RULKENS

HOW TO BECOME SUCCESSFUL AT CLAIMING TIME

CHAPTER 06

Time is a priority. In other words: there's always time, but the thing is, will I prioritize you for using my time? And if you want to use my time, it's important to keep three things in mind.

First of all, connect the event to my strategic goals. In other words: how will this event help me to achieve my strategic goals?

The second important thing is to use my language, the language of outcomes, the language of results, and avoid using the language of processes and details. Because if you use the languages of process and details, I automatically assume you need to talk to my people. It's no longer about strategy. It's about operations and tactics.

And lastly, if you want to use my time, it is important to understand how to use me in your entire process. There are three ways you can use me. First to make decisions. Second to brainstorm ideas and third, to get clarity about goals, but also clarity about boundaries, and options to get to these goals. Now, keep this in mind: connect to strategic goals, use the right language, and use me in your approach efficiently.

That's the way you can claim time.

Take a moment to reflect. Grab a pen.
Jot down the answers to the following questions:

What did you do previously, whereby you were not being taken seriously when event owners were having the conversation about change?

What buttons are you pushing to get what you need?

When asking yourself "Why are people not taking the design process seriously?" what critical behaviours did you demonstrate, that others could have observed? (that got in the way, of what you want

Take a moment ...

REFLECT.

How can you and your team zoom out and empathize with the event owner to address their required outcomes?

Is your event owner not ready or are you as the event designer not ready?

07. —

HAVING THE CONVERSATION

CHAPTER 07

CONVEI

QUESTION TO ASK

Now that you know what you've read in the past chapters and have successfully claimed the time to design you can now have the conversation.

The conversation to address the issue at hand: "design to change".

But before you jump into that, there is an important last question to ask yourself.

How do I apply what I learned, in my next conversation, in order to become a trusted adviser?

The pain question in this chapter is: **Why are good conversations so hard to master?**
The gain question is : **Why are the toughest conversations so valuable?**

Why leave important conversations to chance if they can be anticipated and prepared for?

The likelihood of having worthwhile outcomes is much greater if you consciously prepare and practice.

PRINCIPLES

So this next conversation, you will not leave to chance. You will prepare it and consciously think through the approach you will take and consider the elements that are so critical to its success for both you and your conversational partner.

Let's consider the key elements of good conversations:

- They take time to prepare (why, when, where, how and what)
- They take two or more viewpoints and perspectives to align
- The terms on which they take place are jointly set by both parties
- They are critical in timing
- They take time to practice
- They take courage
- They take risk
- They take grit & perseverance
- They have to come full circle to create value

A conversation addressing a problem doesn't immediately require a solution but is an invitation to explore the problem and what it takes to open the design conversation.

Suppressing the urge to immediately provide an answer but finding the words to be a trusted advisor in every moment. Instead of giving in to the urge to answer, what question could you ask?

For instance, let's pretend your event owner runs into you and asks you about the next event that is now top of mind for them. They fire a direct question at you. "Where should we hold the next sales kickoff for January?".

It's now your choice to fall into the trap of providing a direct answer with a solution or to be the trusted advisor that takes this direct question and flips it into an opportunity. That opportunity to have a prepared conversation about the full scope of the need instead of answering to the urgent want in an unprepared moment.

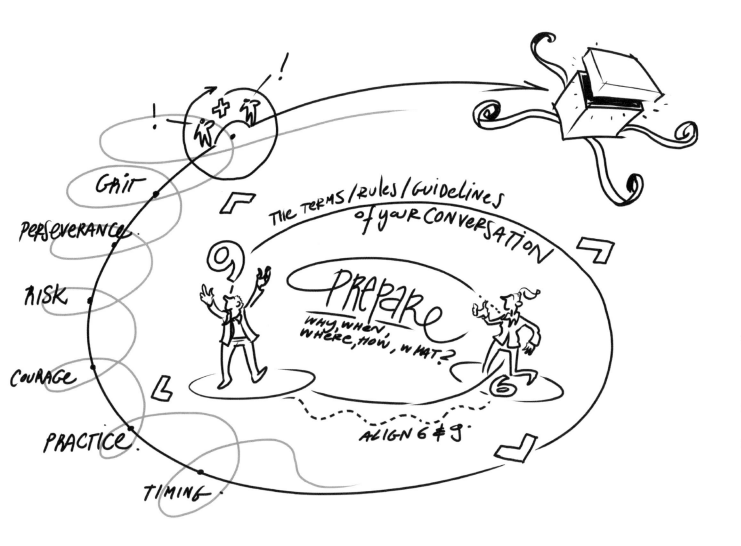

There is no substitute for preparation, practice and simulation. These are the key ingredients to consider when you are looking to improve your conversations. It is a muscle you need to develop. A skillset to master and a mindset to own. You are now in charge and capable to guide the course of action as a result of the good conversations.

You can only be a trusted advisor if you consistently have good conversations and jointly set the terms on when and where they happen. This is what peers do, they respect the time and timing of conversations with each other and are seen as equals regardless of hierarchy.

EACH CONVERSATION IS A MINI-EVENT IN ITSELF.

"WHAT IS AT STAKE?"

"KNOW YOUR AUDIENCE" AND THEIR PREFERENCES. PAGE 165 HANDBOOK.

TIME & GOAL.

PROCESS

Leaving conversations to chance is the last of your intended behaviours. Preparation and practice are your best friends. Failure is acceptable. Key is to keep the relationship with the conversation partner and can acknowledge the failures and learn to build on them together.

What steps can you actually take to prepare the conversation?

1. What stake

Preparing a conversation is like designing a "mini" event. You empathize with the stakeholders, define their entering and exiting behaviours. Address their pains and anticipate their expectations. Then consider their exit behaviour, the gains and what would make them satisfied after the conversation. This will be specifically different for the conversation partners and considering it from both perspectives is important when preparing.

Then consider what they commit to (in time and opportunity cost) for having this conversation. What do they expect in return? What jobs does the conversation help them get done? And what promise have you made to your conversation partner?

Based on the above you think about the experience journey of how this conversation will go. Where will it be? How much time will you both have? What is the order and sequence of the topics you address and discuss. What are the social, emotional and functional ingredients in the why, how and what you discuss?

What questions will be asked and when will they probably come up. As no conversation partners are alike, it's important to empathize with them. What do they see? What are they thinking and feeling? What do they hear you say and

LANGUAGE

_____ wise

_____ intelligent

_____ practical.

→ in yourself

→ your TEAM

→ your PROCESS

TRUST

others say? Ultimately what do they say and do and what pains and gains are associated with this?

2. What preference

In Chapter 7 of the Event Design handbook - Influencing for success - we explored the individual preferences and why it is important to understand these individual behavioural preferences. Is your conversation partner talk-full? Or do they think a lot before talking? Are they concealing with the way the lead or are they revealing? Do they have a preference for action or do they prefer a very logical, methodological approach to the way you address the conversation topic.

It's important to consider the above and consider the circumstances in which they will be, when the conversation is due to take place. The do's and don'ts in these specific conversations are related to the preference of your conversation partner. A way to learn more about these techniques can be found in the LEAD (Logical - Empathy - Action - Difference) model.

3. What time

How much time do you take to prepare each conversation? Does it equate to the importance of what it is you are looking to achieve? Who else would you need to involve in the conversation to get the job done?

4. What language

When having the conversations, it is good practice to use the language to converse in to make yourself understood and to know the hot buttons for the event owner. In each chapter we addressed the executive perspective and their triggers. Below you will find a recap of those components.

EVENT DESIGN
MASTERMIND

MARIE-FRANCE WATSON, CED DES
MANAGER
ACADEMIC AND INTERNATIONAL CONFERENCES, CONCORDIA UNIVERSITY

Collaboration is an accelerator for change, which is what ultimately makes designs better. Conversations are instrumental for good collaboration, yet not easy to master.

A conversation is never formulaic or pre programmed. Careful listening, empathizing and knowing the motivation, triggers and opening up to the other perspective. Your conversation's flow should lead to agreement on the next step. Always have that in mind and stick to it. Don't be tempted to overstretch what one conversation can achieve and build a bridge to the next conversation. Ensure the mutual commitment to have the next conversation between the event designer and the owner.

Even if you regularly fail at achieving the above. Know that sometimes you have to dust yourself off and never give up on having that good conversation. Never jeopardize the relationship because you didn't get what you wanted. Perhaps this is what was needed to understand each other as peers. Perseverance will reward you nicely, as there will always be an opportunity for a next conversation. Embrace this ambiguity and keep the relationship in mind, it's the key to mutual success.

To prepare efficiently, let's review the executive's language preferences of the past chapters. Flip the page for the bullet point overview of questions from the event owner's perspective. This will help you prepare to identify, respond and act.

Having considered the above and prepared adequately, now take on the designer mindset of actually going and doing it. You are equipped with the skills and attitude to crack any problem.

Be courageous and confident. Trust yourself, trust the team, trust the process.

1. HORIZONS OF CHANGE
Vision & Connection
- Do you allow me to express my vision?
  - If we talk about events and if we talk about horizons of change, what is it that we can do to ensure that people adopt this vision?
- How do you enable the connection between my vision and the event?

2. PERSPECTIVE
Risk & Reward
- How are you going to manage the biggest risk of the event?
  - What is it that we're going to do to minimize exposure to risks, which I don't want to see as an event owner?
- How are events positioned as part of an entire program of change
- How would it improve my condition as a leader of this organisation?

3. PROCESS OR OUTCOME
Implicit & Explicit Process Boundaries
- What does success of the event look like?
- How do we know we are successful?
- How will success of the event help me to achieve my strategic goals?

4. WANTS VERSUS NEEDS

Shifting Thinking & Giving Options

- How do you shift my thinking from what I want, because I know what I want to, what I need?
- Are you giving me some freedom in order to get what you say I need? Do you give me options?

5. PUTTING DESIGN ON THE AGENDA

Setting Boundaries and creating leverage

- How do we reach alignment about the guardrails to give the feeling I'm in control?
- How can we leverage what we are doing?
- How to become successful at claiming time

6. CLAIMING TIME

Prioritization and Language

- How will you make me prioritize you, for using my time?
- How will this event help me to achieve my strategic goals?
- How do you maintain the language of outcomes?
- How will you use me in your process (to make decisions, to brainstorm ideas, to get clarity about goals)

"Why are good conversations
so hard to master?"

OUTCOME

A conversation has many unknowns and both parties can influence the outcomes. There is a fine line between the path you would like to see and the path it ultimately takes. You have to be ok with it and be ready to accept its outcomes. It takes two to tango; lead or be led.

In the words of Thomas Bach, President IOC, "You want to be the leader of change and not the object of change".

The gain question is : **Why are the toughest conversations so valuable?**

A tough conversation addresses what people really care about. So if you are able to address that need properly,

you can really touch the nerve or heart of your conversation partner. You might get it wrong or you might get it right. Being right is never the goal. It's about the value the exchange has created for both parties in the intended direction of change.

It takes effort to consider someone else's point of view as a reality. Having addressed the issues and using the right language in the conversation with the event owner, allows you to appreciate their stake. If you do this right, you will have a seat at the table. Not just once but perpetually.

You are now on your way to become a trusted advisor to the event owner as a conversation partner. Sustain the effort and they will see you as a peer.

Tough conversations are so valuable because trusted advisors respect each other in any and every situation. It takes courage to rise to the level of trusted advisorship. It only creates value when used and will regularly be challenged in critical moments of truth. They ultimately are the recognition humans most crave.

08.

'Improve our world, one event at a time!'

YOUR TURN TO DESIGN

CHAPTER 08

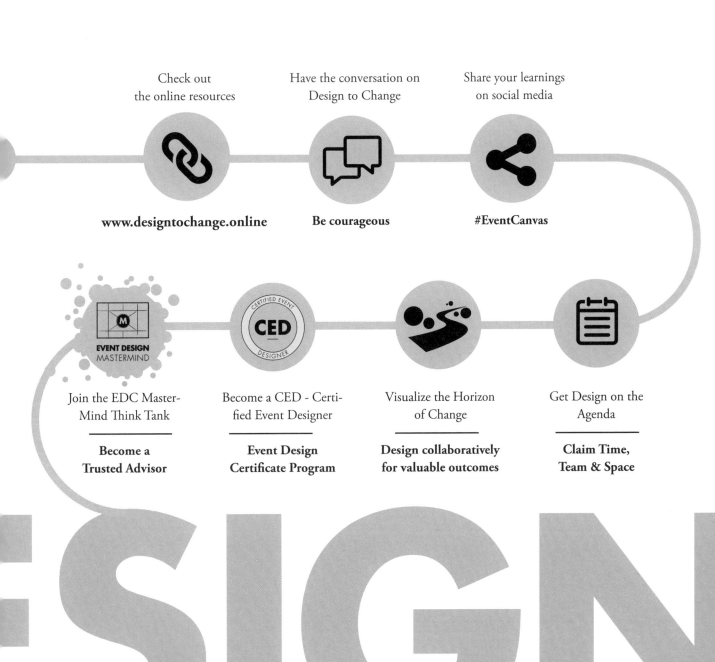

Check out
the online resources

Have the conversation on
Design to Change

Share your learnings
on social media

www.designtochange.online

Be courageous

#EventCanvas

Join the EDC Master-
Mind Think Tank

Become a CED - Certi-
fied Event Designer

Visualize the Horizon
of Change

Get Design on the
Agenda

**Become a
Trusted Advisor**

**Event Design
Certificate Program**

**Design collaboratively
for valuable outcomes**

**Claim Time,
Team & Space**

EVENT DESIGN
MASTERMIND

CED

CERTIFIED EVENT
DESIGNER

163

The last part of this book is dedicated to the Design to Change Glossary of the terminology and concepts you have read and seen in this book.

Besides the Glossary, your purchase of this book unlocks a rich digital space with examples, how to's, worksheets and learnings extracted from the EDC MasterMind Programs and Think Tank sessions. We invite you to join the conversation there and exchange with your fellow Event Designers and Event Owners

EVENT DESIGN
MASTERMIND

ALANA SEIDERS, CED+

MARKETING DIRECTOR
VIVOS THERAPEUTICS, INC.

Design to Change, The Event Design Handbook and the Event Canvas
provide structure and direction while also providing the ability to
create thoughtful and well-planned journeys to create a real change of
Behaviour in the minds of the stakeholders you wish to change. Trust
the process and do the work and you'll achieve the desired outcome.

165

DESIGN TO CHANGE
GLOSSARY

Amplitude: The amount of change that is anticipated upon or achieved in a single event.

Arc of Change: The trajectory taken from the beginning point of the change to the desired end point to achieve the overarching aim. It binds together the narrative storyline of multiple change delta's required to achieve the overarching aim.

Back-casting: Backcasting is a planning method that starts with defining a desirable future and then works backwards to identify policies and programs that will connect that specified future to the present. The fundamental question of backcasting asks: "if we want to attain a certain goal, what actions must be taken to get there?"

Behaviour change: Refers to any transformation or modification of human Behaviour and conduct over time. In this book it pertains to the delta (difference) between the entering behaviour and the exiting behaviour of a stakeholder for an event or series of events.

CED - Certified Event Designer: a practitioner of event design who masters the skills and knowledge required to facilitate and guide Event Design using the Event Canvas Methodology. They are equipped with a full scope of skills and techniques needed to understand and apply the #EventCanvas methodology. They are trained at Level 3 of the Event Design Certificate Program and possess the knowledge, skills and tools to help teams better design their event and elevate the dialogue to include senior stakeholders and event owners. They are confident in articulating how events are designed to create value for its stakeholders.

Delta: The intended change in behaviour of the key stakeholders as a result of attending an event.

Event: Any gathering of two or more people or groups of people (stakeholders) in which their behaviour is changed.

Event Design: The process of articulating change, setting boundaries, and prototyping your event using design thinking and doing.

Event Canvas ™: A visual-thinking tool on a single piece of paper that allows people to articulate how an event creates value. The Event Canvas ™ was developed by Roel Frissen and Ruud Janssen and can be studied further at eventcanvas.org and in the Event Design Handbook published in 2016.

Event Designer: a practitioner of event design

Event Design Community: A community of practitioners of event design.

Event Owner: The proprietor of the Event, often also the initiator of the event. They control whether the event will be held or not.

EDC MasterMind: A community of Certified Event Designers and practitioners of event design who are on a journey to be(come) trusted advisors to their event owners through a series of events and think and do tank activities in that community.

Horizon of Change: Refers to a way to think about the scale of change. A Horizon is the limit to how far you can see into the future and plan for change. Over the Horizon is the unknown; it lies beyond predictability and cannot be planned for. Most importantly, the Horizon defines a goal, and in so doing, aligns the collaborators. It needs to be determined in advance, communicated, and agreed to by all who strive for shared goals.

Flexible Focus: When individuals focus their energies towards a particular end destination, but remain flexible in how they arrive there. Moreover, those who have developed flexible focus are able to find the most effective path towards achievement because an opportunistic mindset naturally arises.

Frequency: the rate at which something occurs over a particular period of time. In this book the frequency of change is when and how often the stepping stones of delta's are planned.

Groupthink: decision making by a group (especially in a manner that discourages creativity or individual responsibility)

Perspective: a particular attitude towards or way of regarding something; a point of view.

Prototype: A prototype is an early sample, model, or release of an event built to test a concept or process. A prototype is generally used to evaluate a new design as an option. Prototyping serves to provide specifications for a real, working system rather than a theoretical one. In some design workflow models, creating a prototype is the step between the formalization and the evaluation of an idea.

Overarching Aim: An overarching general statement of the direction where a team needs to go and what it wants to achieve. It is a direction-finding statement without any specific detail.

Stakeholder: A person or group of people with an interest or concern in an event. They choose to create a part of an event because it is more important to them to participate than to not.

Stakeholder Alignment: Consists of weighing and balancing all of the competing demands by each of those who have a claim on it and bringing them in a position of agreement or alliance. A stakeholder analysis does not preclude the interests of the stakeholders overriding the interests of the other stakeholders affected, but it ensures that all affected will be considered. Stakeholder analysis is frequently used during the preparation phase of a project to assess the attitudes of the stakeholders regarding the potential changes. Stakeholder alignment can be done once or on a regular basis to track changes in stakeholder relationships and assess their power and interest over time.

Stakeholder Alignment Canvas: A visual-thinking tool on a single piece of paper that allows the users to longlist stakeholders, rank them, and arrange them in a matrix of 2 axes: one for power and the other for level of interest. Ultimately, the stakeholder alignment canvas allows users to align a team to the appropriate stakeholder to design form and to identify the overarching aim. The Stakeholder Alignment Canvas was developed by David Bancroft Turner, Roel Frissen, Ruud Janssen and Dennis Luijer.

Timing Conversations: a particular point or period of time when conversations happen.

Trusted Advisor: A person with a sought after proficiency who gives advice and is seen as a peer by the one seeking advice.

Zoom in - Zoom out: This refers to being adept at switching among different horizons throughout the design process, being clear about where you are, and making sure everyone else is shifting scope together. Communicating with the terms Zoom In and Zoom Out acknowledges several things: that there are different scales of focus; that there are identifiable increments of change along the path to more distant goals of behaviour changes; and that the concept of Horizons provides the language to communicate with colleagues about how the scope of the current Horizon fits into other Horizons.

REFERENCES

Roel Frissen, Ruud Janssen, Dennis Luijer. *Event Design Handbook, Systematically Design Innovative Events using the Event Canvas.* BIS Publishing 2016.

Rensis Likert. *New Patterns of Management.* McGraw-Hill 1987.

Dennis Luijer, *Drawing Out Change.* Event Design Collective GmbH 2020.

Joseph Pine & James Gilmore. *The Experience Economy; Competing for Customer Time, Attention, and Money.* Harvard Business Review Press 2019.

Paul Rulkens. *The Power of Preeminence.* Vakmedianet 2017.

Marc Stickdorn, Markus Hirmess, Adam Lawrence, Jakob Schneider. *This is Service Design Doing.* O'Reilly Media 2018.

Edward N. Zalta, *The Stanford Encyclopedia of Philosophy*, The Metaphysics Research Lab. Center for the Study of Language and Information. Stanford University.

EDC MasterMind - Amsterdam, The Netherlands 2019, Online 2020 - *https://edco.global/mastermind/*

Travis Avery AR Logo from the Noun Project

Alexander Skowalsky Landscape from the Noun Project

Alice Design Agenda from the Noun Project

Shashank Singh Conversation from the Noun Project

ACKNOWLEDGEMENTS
& SPECIAL THANKS

RAW CONVERSATIONS DISTILLED INTO ACTIONABLE APPROACHES.

It probably doesn't surprise you that just like our first book, events were the root cause of this book.

Driven by the needs and conversations with Event Owners and Event Designers who use the Event Canvas™ around the world, we have written the "DESIGN to Change" book as a companion to the "Event Design Handbook" first published in 2016.

Thousands have been trained in the Event Design Certificate (EDC) Programs. Since its inception in 2015, we have collaborated with over 500 CED Certified Event Designer candidates on an individual basis in the 30 cohorts of the Level 3 EDC Program. Enabling others to facilitate Event Design, we have observed that candidates are able to master the Event Canvas ™ methodology in practice, yet claiming time from the team and getting permission from the event owner to design can be daunting.

Based on our experiences in our consulting practice and coaching Certified Event Designers (CED'ers) to be confident in these conversations, we have distilled and articulated successful practices in this book.

The conversations and stories of these experiences were the foundation of this book.

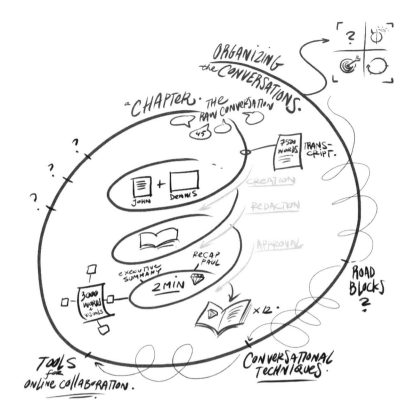

The book was written after a series of multi-layered raw conversations between Roel Frissen, Ruud Janssen and Dennis Luijer.

The raw conversations were recorded and transcribed identifying roadblocks, conversational topics and techniques using tools for online collaboration. The raw conversations between the authors were then distilled back to legible chapters by our editor John Loughlin. The rhythm of 4 elements in each chapter allowed Dennis to visualize the essence of the conversations in 2D with his sharp pen and unique style. The book's structure and approach was first presented as a concept to the team at the Event Design Collective. Subsequently the visual and written words were reassembled into a prototype of the book.

The prototype was the backbone of event design of the EDC MasterMind program in November 2020. What started with recorded personalised podcasts led to conversations about pivotal moments of change.

Conversation labs were held challenging the EDC MasterMinds to practice and sharpen their skills in actual conversations with event owners.

In practicing these conversational skills and approaches, each element addressed in the book was experienced in the instructional design of the 3 day event. What the participants didn't know was that each of them subsequently received a personalized hard copy of the alpha draft version of the book during the third day of the EDC MasterMind Program in November 2020.

Over Christmas, the EDC MasterMinds were surprised by an extra audio experience of the content. Colleague Anthony Vade, recorded the audio-book version of the alpha of the book for the EDC MasterMinds to listen to whilst reviewing the book's first 6 chapters.

Meanwhile, Paul Rulkens, our EDC MasterMind ringleader and Trusted Advisor took every chapter and narrated an Executive Perspective of the topic at hand in that chapter now from the Event Owner's point of view.

A systematic review of the first version of the book chapters was then planned with the EDC MasterMinds who contributed to sharpening the alpha version into its current version.

In that process, the most committed EDC MasterMinds were asked to also contribute their perspective which you have found highlighted in the book.

The review of the first prototype of this book was made possible by:

Alana Seiders, CED	Gerrit Jessen, CMP, CMM, CED	Naomi Love, CED
Amy Badersnider, CED	Ingrid Rip, CED	Patti Spaniola, CED
Andrea Vernengo, CED	Jayr Bass	Stefanie Simmons, CED
Angeles Moreno, CED	Joël Letang	Tanya Spournova, CED
Anthony Vade, CED	Luca Vernengo, CED	Vincent Roux, CED
Chanet Ham, CED	Marie-France Watson, CED	Werner Puchert, CED
Erno Ovaska, CED	Marga Groot Zwaaftink, CED	
Frank Dräger, CED	Mauricio Magdaleno, CED	

We also acknowledged that true conversations are to be had live and in rich content formats, hence our decision to augment the content of this book with a commitment to providing examples, tools, resources and experiences on the digital platform connected to the book.

The layout and production of the book has been done by Giovanni de Reus and Frank Bakker based on the design and layout of the previous book styled by Cristel Lit.

This book would not have been possible if it were not for the countless individuals (you know who you are as you are reading this) who contributed to the conversations about events, event design and the horizon of change.

Credit goes to our moms and dads, spouses, siblings and friends who have fostered and challenged our curiosity along our journeys to put pen to paper for this book. Their support means the world to us and the pivotal moments make for lasting memories.

We encourage you to go out and have courageous conversations. If you find someone else sees things differently, be curious, ask a question. Try asking: "I never thought about it exactly that way before. What can you share that would help me see what you see?" What's remarkable about curiosity conversations is that the people you are curious about tend to become curious about what drives you.

Listen well, take copious notes and share your feedback with fellow event design enthusiasts by using the #EventCanvas to tag your conversations. By sharing our experiences in rich conversations, we trust this book can make us all better conversationalists for change.

We hope this book enriches you with a collection of new perspectives, a new way of navigating conversations, and a whole set of new stories and experiences to share.

Most grateful for our next conversations,

Dennis Luijer, Paul Rulkens, Roel Frissen, Ruud Janssen

MEET
THE AUTHORS

RUUD JANSSEN
@ruudwjanssen

Ruud is an international speaker, facilitator and designer of high stakes conferences & events. He helps organisations innovate by thinking differently based on functional, social and technological advancements using business and event model innovation. He created the Event Canvas™ with Roel Frissen to enable teams to systematically design events that matter.
Ruud is the co-founder of Event Design Collective GmbH, the event design consulting & training firm.

DENNIS LUIJER
@visiblethinking

As a Design Engineer Dennis believes in the powerful practice of visualization and its ability to MAKE CHANGE VISIBLE. His role in visualising how events create value, brings the strategic narrative to life and ties the event story to each individual contribution that realizes the design goal of behaviour change. As co-founder of the Event Design Collective GmbH he works constantly to improve & design new visual tools that help event professionals to engage and design extraordinary Events.

ROEL FRISSEN
@roelfrissen

Roel is an entrepreneur, speaker, facilitator, non-executive, and trusted advisor for organisations. He helps professionals to engage their colleagues and clients in strategic conversations and design projects. On a quest to create a common and visual language to ease the conversation between Event Planner and Event Owner, he created together with Ruud Janssen the Event Canvas™. Roel is the co-founder of Event Design Collective GmbH, the event design consulting & training firm.

VISIT

www.designtochange.online